Reducing Crime and assuring Justice

June 1972: A Statement on National Policy
by the Research and Policy Committee

 of the Committee
for Economic Development

Single copy ... $1.50

Printed in U.S.A.
First Printing June 1972
Design: Harry Carter
Library of Congress Catalog Card Number: 72-81298
International Standard Book Number: 0-87186-046-5

Committee for Economic Development
477 Madison Avenue, New York, N.Y. 10022

CONTENTS

102707

THE RESPONSIBILITY FOR
CED STATEMENTS ON NATIONAL POLICY

This statement has been approved for publication as a statement of the Research and Policy Committee by the members of that Committee and of the Committee for Improvement of Management in Government, subject to individual dissents or reservations noted herein. The trustees who are responsible for this statement are listed on the opposite page. Company associations are included for identification only; the companies do not share in the responsibility borne by the individuals.

The Research and Policy Committee is directed by CED's bylaws to:
"Initiate studies into the principles of business policy and of public policy which will foster the full contribution by industry and commerce to the attainment and maintenance of high and secure standards of living for people in all walks of life through maximum employment and high productivity in the domestic economy."

The bylaws emphasize that:

"All research is to be thoroughly objective in character, and the approach in each instance is to be from the standpoint of the general welfare and not from that of any special political or economic group."

The Research and Policy Committee is composed of 60 Trustees from among the 200 businessmen and educators who comprise the Committee for Economic Development. It is aided by a Research Advisory Board of leading economists, a small permanent Research Staff, and by advisors chosen for their competence in the field being considered.

Each Statement on National Policy is preceded by discussions, meetings, and exchanges of memoranda, often stretching over many months. The research is undertaken by a subcommittee, with its advisors. For this statement the Committee for Improvement of Management in Government acted as a subcommittee. Together with the full Research and Policy Committee, CIMG participated in the drafting of findings and recommendations.

Except for the members of the Research and Policy Committee and of CIMG, the recommendations presented herein are not necessarily endorsed by other Trustees or by the advisors, contributors, staff members, or others associated with CED.

The Research and Policy Committee offers these Statements on National Policy as an aid to clearer understanding of the steps to be taken in achieving sustained growth of the American economy. The Committee is not attempting to pass on any pending specific legislative proposals; its purpose is to urge careful consideration of the objectives set forth in the statement and of the best means of accomplishing those objectives.

4

1. Voted to approve the policy statement but submitted memoranda of comment, reservation, or dissent, or wished to be associated with memoranda of others. See pages 75-77.
2. Did not participate in the voting on this statement because of absence from the country.

FOREWORD

The interest of the Committee in crime and justice stems not only from the economic fact that crime costs the business community an estimated $16 billion a year and boosts prices paid by the consumer. Far more important, crime undermines the very basis of American society. It creates fear and destroys the mutual trust and confidence which are the foundation of a healthy nation.

This statement offers no facile solutions, no miraculous nostrums to alleviate a perplexing and pervasive problem. Over the past forty years many commissions have studied these questions, many important recommendations have been made, yet many of the problems they have uncovered remain unsolved. The major contribution of this statement, therefore, does not lie in the individual proposals dealing with the courts, prosecution, police, and corrections. For the Committee believes that important as they are, piecemeal efforts to reform the highly fragmented, patchwork structure of criminal justice will inevitably fail.

The problem is deeper. The Committee believes that the ineffectiveness of the present structure is rooted in the organizational and administrative chaos that characterizes the nation's uncoordinated system of criminal justice, and in the management weaknesses prevailing in agencies at all levels. The Committee therefore proposes a complete administrative overhaul of the criminal justice system and a redistribution of responsibilities, functions, and financial support among the various levels of government. Local governments would be relieved of all obligations other than maintenance of urban police forces, and each state would draw together all criminal justice activities under a strong, centralized Depart-

7

ment of Justice. The federal role would be concentrated in a new, independent Federal Authority To Ensure Justice, which would coordinate the fight against crime on the national level and would provide strong financial incentives for the reorganization of state and local systems.

Although the Committee focused on the *administration* of justice, we recognize that crime is not an alien, isolated phenomenon. Crime is deeply rooted in the social ills of our society. Over the years this Committee has made extensive and concrete recommendations for major changes in the areas of welfare reform, urban education, and job and training programs, and is currently studying needed changes in housing and health care. The Committee's proposals dealing with these vital issues should be implemented for reasons quite apart from our belief that they would ameliorate conditions breeding delinquency and crime.

The trustees and advisors who participated in developing the proposed solutions brought high qualifications of experience and insight to bear on them, but, in addition, help was obtained from many outside sources. We are especially grateful to Earl Warren, James V. Bennett, Ramsey Clark, David Fogel, Ernest C. Friesen, Bernard L. Garmire, Milton G. Rector, Charles H. Rogovin, Dr. Jesse Rubin, and James Q. Wilson.

CED's Committee for Improvement of Management in Government (CIMG) prepared this report under the able chairmanship of Wayne E. Thompson. Earlier development of such policy statements as *Modernizing Local Government, Modernizing State Government, Reshaping Government in Metropolitan Areas,* and *Making Congress More Effective* built a solid foundation for inquiry into crime and the administration of justice.

The Research and Policy Committee extends its thanks to Wayne E. Thompson and the members of CIMG, its advisory boards, and the many other eminent authorities who participated in this project. We recognize as well the research and drafting contributions of Robert F. Steadman, Director, and Mary E. Baluss of the CIMG staff, and the editorial assistance of Jacob Worenklein, CED's Associate Director of Information.

We express our gratitude to the Carnegie Corporation, the Rockefeller Brothers Fund, the Kellogg Foundation, and other foundations and donors for their generous financial support.

Philip M. Klutznick, *Co-Chairman*
Research and Policy Committee

1.

INTRODUCTION

PROMPT, equitable, and effective administration of justice is the first responsibility of a civilized society. The Constitution recognizes this fact in its preamble: "We, the people of the United States, in order to form a more perfect union, establish justice, insure domestic tranquility . . ." Long neglect of this priority at state and other governmental levels is in itself a major source of lawlessness, disorder, and alienation.

Crime running rampant is certainly not the mark of a healthy society. Large-scale criminal activity, whether organized or spontaneous, undermines an economy based upon opportunity and enterprise, while it fosters a sense of injustice among the poor and the minorities. No citizen can justify indifference, least of all members of the business community with their special concern for public safety. Complacency will prove suicidal.

Crimes of violence, crimes against property, and white collar crimes have reached intolerable levels. Increases have been extremely high in recent years, and they continue. Crime statistics are incomplete and not very reliable, but the FBI's *Uniform Crime Reports* show a *doubling,* from three million in 1965 to six million in 1971, in the seven categories of serious crime which form the basis of the FBI's Crime Index (murder, forcible rape, robbery, aggravated assault, burglary, larceny $50 and over, auto theft).[1] Worse, these numbers are under-stated.[2]

Events of the past decade have intensified the challenge to order and justice. Drug abuse is rising rapidly, terroristic violence is now a fact of life, and crime syndicates flourish. More and more Americans hesitate to venture upon the streets, especially at night; they feel inse-cure even within their own homes. Almost two-thirds of all women and nearly half of all men say they were "more afraid and uneasy" on the streets in 1971 than in 1970. Conditions around the Capitol, the White House, and the UN headquarters have embarrassed the nation. Crime has long been much more common in the United States than in other industrialized countries, but it has now passed the limits of tolerance.

Business leadership is needed as never before in a cooperative effort to control and reverse present trends. The special involvement of business is twofold. Organized crime exacts an annual toll of billions of dollars in truck hijackings, inventory losses, "disappearance" of securi-ties, extortions, and inroads into legitimate enterprise. Such costs have to be passed on, ultimately, to consumers and investors, as are the rising burdens of shoplifting and internal business thefts.

But the chief anxiety is not with these losses, serious though they are. Violence and property losses have reached levels that destroy the confidence and trust upon which American social and economic insti-tutions are founded, menacing national prosperity and strength. We believe these trends can be reversed, but not without mounting a deter-mined, cooperative effort to remove grave defects in the administration of criminal justice by such means as this Committee advocates.

The object of this statement is to examine the administration of criminal justice in this country and to propose measures urgently needed

---

[1] See Appendix A for data concerning the increase in these seven categories and for esti-mates of arrests in all crimes and offenses.

[2] Only murders and auto thefts are well reported. Research surveys reveal that barely two-thirds of all robberies are reported; half to three-fourths of rapes, assaults, bur-glaries and larcenies remain unknown to the police. Statistics on less serious crimes are even less dependable, but the FBI estimates arrests for them at seven million annually (excluding minor traffic offenses). Moreover, actual offenses committed number five to ten times the arrests made for them.

10

to correct its deficiencies. We view these changes as imperative, while recognizing the importance of other approaches to the prevention of juvenile delinquency and adult criminal conduct. The physical and social environment has deep relevance to human behavior, of course, but only brief reference to such considerations is within the scope of this statement of public policy which is focused on the legal and administrative aspects of criminal justice.

Deeper Causes of Crime

Although many factors associated with high crime rates have been identified, uncertainties still surround the cause and effect relationships in criminal conduct. It is clear, however, that crime as a total problem cannot and should not be viewed in isolation from other great social and behavioral dilemmas. The highest crime rates, five to ten times those for rural areas, are found in the congested centers of great cities, in association with a long list of other social ills. Housing there is generally substandard, often unfit for habitation; unemployment is endemic, especially among the young; health and sanitation services are weak; many of the public schools are demoralized, with heavy drop-out rates; and deep poverty is pervasive.

Relatively high rates of juvenile delinquency have occurred consistently over a long period of time in central city slum areas, regardless of their racial and ethnic constituencies. Delinquent behavior is often considered "normal" and socially acceptable there, while nondelinquent behavior may seem abnormal. Many parents strive to overcome these influences, but family and social sanctions are ineffective against peer-group support for unlawful conduct. Spontaneous criminality and easy recruitment by organized syndicates frequently result.

Nationwide, over half of all those arrested for the seven Index crimes are under 19 years of age; one-fifth are 14 or younger. About one-sixth of all males aged 12 to 17 are arrested for some crime (in addition to minor traffic offenses) every year; over the next six years there will be an average of one such arrest for each member of this group. Rapid recent growth in the 15-24 age bracket (47 per cent in the 1960's and continuing in the 1970's) explains perhaps one-fourth of the recent crime increases, in view of a disproportionate involvement by this group in most kinds of offenses. Half of those arrested for the four violent crimes mentioned, and one-third of those arrested for the three crimes against property, are blacks. Black victimization rates are also extremely high, especially in the ghettos.

Without making more specific recommendations, we do support immediate intensification and expansion of scientific inquiries into these social and behavioral aspects of criminal conduct. The findings should be actively tested, without hindering or delaying the actions needed to achieve prompt, effective, and equitable *administration* of criminal justice. Meanwhile, extensive and concrete recommendations for major changes made by this Committee within the last few years in the fields of urban education, employment, and welfare should also be implemented—for reasons quite apart from our belief that they would ameliorate conditions that help breed delinquency and crime.[3]

It must be recognized that two important developments of recent years are beyond the customary bounds of criminological research. One is social alienation and rejection of "establishment" values on the part of a significant segment of the nation's well-educated youth. In some cases this has been carried to revolutionary extremes; it has also found expression in approval of theft, vandalism, and drug abuse as acceptable means to assault or reject the existing social structure. Moreover, militancy within minority groups has grown, notably but not exclusively among blacks. The frequency of violent confrontation between alienated groups and the police has risen; the intensity of reciprocal animosities is all too evident.

Much bitterness and disaffection stem from the widespread conviction that American criminal codes and their administration are unfair, inequitable, and—in a word—unjust. The sense of justice is a basic human need. Any society rests upon insecure foundations if it contains major elements that believe its laws and the manner of their administration are unjust. Yet, injustice does exist; there is discriminatory enforcement of unpopular laws, police corruption, inordinate court delay, and brutality in the prisons. Our institutions are defective.

---

[3] See the CED Research and Policy Committee's Statements on National Policy: *Innovation in Education* (July 1968); *Improving the Public Welfare System* (April 1970); *Training and Jobs for the Urban Poor* (July 1970); *Education for the Urban Disadvantaged* (March 1971); *Social Responsibilities of Business Corporations* (June 1971). See also CED Supplementary Papers: *Functional Education for Disadvantaged Youth* (March 1971); *Resources for Urban Schools* (May 1971); and *The Conditions for Educational Equality* (July 1971). Policy statements concerning housing needs and health care are currently under consideration.

Defective Institutions

A reluctance to face the facts has worsened matters. Reaction has been slow and weak at every governmental level, most of all in the 50 states which have primary responsibility. Criminal codes are badly out-of-date; enforcement is fragmented; prosecutors make improper use of plea bargaining; court congestion degrades the judicial process; and prisons are schools for crime. High officials too often seem oblivious to signs of widespread, deep-seated official corruption.

Every aspect of the "non-system" of criminal justice is in dire need of modernization; piecemeal tinkering will not help much. More arrests create complications where jails are overcrowded and courts are clogged with long-standing unsettled cases. More judges and prosecuting attorneys avail little while correctional institutions have no room for those convicted and sentenced. Doubling the number of prison cells of the kind now in use is a dubious expedient when two-thirds of those released return within a few months, convicted of new crimes.

A total, all-embracing "systems" overhaul of the present "non-system" of criminal justice is an absolute necessity. A "systems approach" as outlined in chapter 8 calls for clarification of objectives, and for development of a complete design involving every interrelated variable affecting the intended outcomes. Sweeping reforms can be enacted and put into effect, but only with a full public commitment to basic changes.

The nation has been well advised of its needs. A series of Presidential Commissions composed of distinguished and knowledgeable citizens has studied these problems, analyzed and reported upon them at length.[4] Their recommendations over a period of 40 years display a

---

[4] For a comparison of recommendations made by four commissions, see forthcoming CED Supplementary Paper, *Better Management of the Criminal Justice System* (1972). A chapter by Mary E. Baluss compares recommendations concerning the police, the courts, and corrections made by the National Commission on Law Observance and Enforcement (Wickersham Commission), 1931; the President's Commission on Law Enforcement and Administration of Justice (Katzenbach Commission), 1967; the National Advisory Commission on Civil Disorders (Kerner Commission), 1968; and the National Commission on the Causes and Prevention of Violence (Eisenhower Commission), 1969. In addition to the reports by these four Commissions, see also the reports of the President's Committee on Juvenile Delinquency and Youth Crime (1961), the Attorney General's Committee on Poverty and the Administration of Federal Criminal Justice (1963), the President's Commission on Crime in the District of Columbia (1966), the National Commission on the Reform of Federal Criminal Laws (1971), the Advisory Commission on Intergovernmental Relations *(State-Local Relations in the Criminal Justice System,* 1971), and the American Bar Association.

13

remarkable degree of consistency and similarity. But beginning with the renowned Wickersham Commission (1929-1931) few of these recommendations have been adopted—even in part—although repeated, reinforced, and expanded in the past decade by thoroughly competent groups that have explored every aspect of criminal administration. A suitable agenda for action has thus been available for 40 years. Most of the detailed proposals made in this statement conform in summary fashion with these prior studies, although we also urge new governmental changes and courses of action to produce the desired results. It is now time to take effective action.

One major obstacle to broad national reform lies in the complex nature of American federalism as it relates to crime and justice, making evasion of responsibility easy.[5] Citizens who desire better protection for persons and property become confused over which level of government or which agencies are primarily at fault. Wherever they turn, they find a resistance to change traditional in both bureaucratic and political circles. The result is continuing deterioration—a trend that must be reversed, promptly and decisively, to secure a viable society.

The main constitutional responsibility for crime prevention and control rests upon the states, an assignment they have botched. They have failed to keep their criminal codes up-to-date, and they have turned responsibility for enforcement over to a welter of overlapping counties, municipalities, townships, and special districts. Despite the obvious and urgent need, the states have neither straightened out their tangled and ineffective patterns of local government nor assumed direct responsibility for law enforcement.

State police are few in number and limited in jurisdiction. Most prosecutions are entrusted to county officials; only three states have taken over this function. Court systems are supported in part by the states and in larger part by counties and other local units, down to magistrate courts and rural justices of the peace. Imprisonment for major offenses is mainly a state function, but local units provide jails and probation officers. *The sanctions of the state criminal codes are applied, therefore, without consistency, uniformity, or effectiveness.*

The criminal justice apparatus of the national government is superior to that of the average state on most counts. Its share of the total burden has always been minor, however, although the list of federal

---

[5] See Appendix B for a detailed, functional breakdown by governmental levels for the several aspects of criminal justice.

crimes has lengthened greatly in recent years. The national judiciary is superior in the quality of its bench, in its unity and central management, in its procedures and sentencing arrangements. The United States Attorneys, while not wholly free from partisan politics, are subject to a degree of central supervision and are better qualified than most of the 3,000 elective and autonomous county prosecutors. While imperfect, the federal prison system is *relatively* enlightened and well-managed. In a similar sense the several federal police forces are *comparatively* well-qualified, well-trained, and well-led.

In 1968 the national government initiated a new approach, providing grants-in-aid to strengthen state and local administrative operations. Unfortunately, this legislation was defective and its execution half-hearted. The hard fact is that the combined efforts of all levels of government have failed to prevent rising tides of crime. In other words, the "federal system" as it presently functions in the field of criminal justice is ineffective; it has broken down.

There is a dilemma here. Past experience indicates that few if any of the 50 states will, either on their own behalf or through their local units, take the wide range of measures needed to meet the present crisis. Yet the constitutional power to make essential changes resides almost entirely in the states; neither national nor local governments have legal authority to act independently of them. New means of national policy formulation, bolstered by incentives powerful enough to energize the states, must therefore be established before substantial progress can be made.

The Rational Solution

After examining many alternatives, we have concluded that by far the best solution lies in creation of a new and independent national agency—a permanent *Federal Authority To Ensure Justice*—funded to contribute half of all state and local costs for police, prosecution, judicial, and correctional agencies meeting basic standards to be set by this Authority.* The Authority would encourage each state to establish *a unified state department of justice* to tie together and provide effective management of functions now performed by separate state agencies

*See Memorandum by MR. HERMAN L. WEISS, page 75.

and by fragmented, weakly organized local units of government. Justification for this major recommendation is set forth in the final chapter of this statement.

There is nothing novel about conditional grants-in-aid; Congressional appropriations for such purposes approach $40 billion, including relatively small sums for law enforcement. Three elements in our proposal are new, however: the scale of available funding; insistence upon high standards in the administration of criminal justice; and independence for the managing Authority, elevating its status over the complex of existing federal agencies and above all state and local instrumentalities. Only in this fashion can crucial weaknesses be overcome; only by this means will a coherent and comprehensive systems approach to the nationwide problems of crime and injustice be possible.

We are well aware of the potential impact upon the U.S. Treasury. If these financial arrangements had been in effect in 1971, with all elements of the criminal justice system as they then were, the added federal burden would have been about $5 billion. On the other hand, state-local expenditures would have been *lowered* by that amount, thus reducing pressures on property and sales taxes. Some of the improvements urged in this statement for future years involve increased costs, at least in the short run. Under present financial arrangements, the main part of these increases would be borne at state-local levels; under our plan the national government would share equally in them.

The basic problem is not financial; the cost of a model system of criminal justice is easily within the means of the American people. It would cost much less than the present burden of crime—estimated at $16 billion yearly for the crimes against business alone, and several times that sum over-all. Public expenditures for criminal justice are now rising after a long period of deprivation, but they were only $7.3 billion in fiscal 1969; private expenditures for insurance and protective measures are estimated to have been $2.7 billion. Thus, the combined public and private total was about $10 billion, or roughly one per cent of the gross national product (GNP). Comparable nationwide outlays were six or seven times that great for health services ($67.2 billion) and for education ($60.5 billion).

This nation can bear the costs essential to assure criminal justice far better than it can afford the consequences of maladministration and injustice. Additional resources will be needed to carry out some of our recommendations, although it would be erroneous to assume that money alone will overcome these problems. Money wasted or mis-

16

directed could compound the difficulties. Hence, our specific proposals concerning the courts, prosecution, police, corrections, and the criminal codes are intended to obtain the most effective use of allocated funds. Most citizens want a sound solution and are quite willing to pay whatever it may cost. They lack a full understanding, however, of the changes that are most necessary.

The two deep-seated sources of current crisis conditions are clear enough: absence of any coherent over-all design, resulting from confusion of powers and responsibilities among the several federal levels of government; and weak, ineffective management of agencies at all levels. **We believe that adoption of our proposal for a Federal Authority To Ensure Justice—properly managed, staffed, and funded—would lead this country toward reversal of the disastrous trends of recent years. The states, through unified departments of justice and other means proposed in this statement, would be encouraged to meet high standards in fulfillment of their constitutional obligations.**

* * * *

An orderly and just society is not an easy goal, nor is it impossible of attainment. It is a goal that must be achieved, and soon, to restore the faith of Americans in their most basic institutions. Means suited to these ends are at hand; adoption depends only upon better public understanding, and upon determined support from the great majority of citizens and opinion leaders.

2

VITALIZING THE COURTS

THE COURTS are the key to order with justice; weakness there undermines the legitimacy of a democratic society. In simplest terms, the objective of any court system should be to assure prompt and even-handed dispensation of civil and criminal justice within the framework of the laws. American courts have another distinctive obligation—to see that the laws and the manner of their administration fall within the boundaries set by national and state constitutions.

Chief Justice Warren E. Burger of the U.S. Supreme Court has recalled the warning by Dean Pound in 1906 that the work of the courts in the twentieth century could not be carried on with the methods and machinery of the nineteenth century. Yet not many changes have been made. Antiquated, rigid procedures encourage delay. Modern techniques are seldom used in managing court operations, although systems planning could be readily applied.

Immediate elimination of delay has first priority among the several major changes needed. Article VI of the Bill of Rights provides that "In all criminal prosecutions, the accused shall enjoy the right to a speedy and public trial . . ." This basic principle, that justice delayed is justice denied, conforms with the axiom that both celerity and certainty are essential to give punishment strong deterrent effect. Some courts hold this view so firmly that they have begun to release prisoners held for unreasonable periods without opportunity for trial.

18

Congestion of court calendars, particularly in the larger cities, is at unacceptable levels nearly everywhere. Civil cases proliferate because of the increasing complexity of modern life—exemplified by urbanization, the use of motor vehicles, and the growth of corporate enterprise. But the criminal caseload also doubled in the 1960's. Moreover, certain otherwise commendable Supreme Court decisions, such as those assuring legal counsel for defendants at all stages, have slowed court processes. The practice of criminal law is financially unattractive; the scarcity of lawyers available both for defense and prosecution forces repeated postponements.

The combined criminal case backlog in the 89 federal district courts rose 18 per cent in fiscal 1970, and was 172 per cent higher than in 1960. In 11 districts, over one-third of the cases had been pending for a year or more. Yet, the number of federal criminal cases is minor compared with those brought before state and local courts—where much longer delays are encountered.

Court congestion can be relieved in two ways—through better management of case schedules, and by creation of additional judgeships. Both can and should be undertaken concurrently. Better management, which should be the first objective, has produced a 58 per cent reduction in backlogs in the New York City Criminal Court, without any addition of money or staff, through adoption of recommendations made by the Economic Development Council of New York City—a group of concerned business leaders. After all possibilities for more efficiency have been exhausted, however, there are many cases where more judges and additional supporting personnel are essential; rising civil caseloads serve to reinforce the point. Effective action in both spheres (and in revision of criminal codes to shorten the list of criminal offenses) must depend upon changing attitudes within the judiciaries, determined executive leadership, and prompt legislative response to calls for funds as well as for statutory and constitutional revisions.

The state legislatures have been slow to provide the additional judgeships, supporting staffs, and adjunct facilities needed; they have done little to encourage better management. Judges are often hesitant in their requests for legislative action. Amounts spent are relatively low; in 1969 total expenditures for all courts—federal, state, and local—were barely one billion dollars. This total is rising, but is still small compared with financial and social losses resulting from an over-burdened judiciary. It is not sound public policy to scrimp on the courts.

19

Enough federal and state judgeships must be created and filled to permit immediate trial of all felony cases and to eliminate time pressures that force plea bargains.*

When the issue is in doubt, the decision should be to enlarge the bench, since growing populations and civil caseloads will soon justify additions. Every judiciary should be adequately funded, with appropriate salaries and tenure for necessary staffs as well as for judges, and with essential equipment provided. All judges should serve full-time and, at the very least, be qualified by license to practice law.

The courts suffer from serious deficiencies other than those directly related to congestion. Political considerations are often a major barrier to creation of necessary additional judgeships at all levels. On the frequent occasions when a chief executive and the legislative body are of different political parties or otherwise at odds, an executive request for additions is likely to be held hostage in bargaining on the prospective appointments or on other unrelated issues. An atmosphere of spoils then surrounds the new judgeships.

Partisan politics influences, and often controls, the selection of judges at local, state, and national levels—a fact which may be explained, but not justified, as a holdover from the Jacksonian period in American politics. In 17 of the 50 highest state courts the justices are elected on partisan ballots and in 12 others on nonpartisan ballots. Most other state and local judges are also elected by partisan ballot. Party nominations are obtained and campaigns financed in ways that tend to discredit both the bar and the judiciary. There is convincing evidence that judgeships have been bought through large campaign or other contributions, especially in major cities.[1]

Partisan politics has no legitimate role in the selection of judges. Emphasis on merit makes executive appointment of judges, under procedures designed to secure high quality and to minimize partisanship, greatly preferable to election.

Newer state constitutions give governors a larger role in selection of judges, sometimes in collaboration with nominating commissions or subject to subsequent ratification at the polls. There is progress toward insistence upon higher qualifications for state and local judges, but it has been slow and sporadic. Although the federal judiciary is appointive, with life tenure and suitable compensation, almost all appointees are members of the President's political party and subject

---

[1] See Martin and Susan Tolchin, *To the Victor* (New York: Random House, 1971).
*See Memorandum by MR. ALEXANDER L. STOTT, page 76.

to various partisan clearances. Executive appointments always involve political considerations since credit or blame will result, but the political process functions at both high and low levels; judicial selections should be on the highest of planes.

This Committee examined the problems of state-local courts five years ago.[2] We proposed measures to overcome grave deficiencies: the multiplicity of trial courts at state, county, city, and township levels; the lack of coherent centralized administrative management; the absence of adequate financial support; the weak arrangements for removal of unqualified or incapacitated judges; and failure to condition federal aid upon major structural revisions. In the past five years progress has been made in some states in judicial compensation and in selection or removal procedures; stronger central management and partial unifications are found in a few cases. But no state has completely overhauled its judiciary, although crime rates have escalated everywhere.

Our earlier recommendations appear to be strongly supported by those best informed about the condition of the American judiciary, and especially by those who have given careful consideration to measures that would minimize the worst difficulties. The new National Center for State Courts may well encourage reforms. The work of the American Bar Association, and of several state bar associations, deserves special commendation.

Each of the 50 states should consolidate all state and local courts into a single judicial branch and assume full responsibility for its financial support.

The opposite arrangement now predominates, with local units compelled to contribute to support of lower state courts while carrying all costs of local courts. In fiscal 1969, local governments spent $660 million on courts, the 50 states only $236 million. Since the laws being enforced are almost exclusively those of the states, the only logical exception to total unification at state expense would be to allow local courts or quasi-judicial agencies to handle minor traffic violations and enforcement of other local ordinances.

Within the consolidated system, court specialization for sensitive and expeditious handling of distinct types of cases could and should be encouraged; the new District of Columbia court for family affairs and Chicago's successful traffic court are two appropriate examples.

---

[2] *Modernizing State Government,* A Statement on National Policy by the Research and Policy Committee, Committee for Economic Development (July 1967).

21

Assignment of cases to judges should be beyond the influence of litigant attorneys, of course, and the same judge should carry each case through from beginning to conclusion.

Central administrative authority over each judiciary should be placed in the hands of its chief justice, advised by a judicial council and acting through a court administrator directly responsible to him.

He should have power to assign judges from one area or court subdivision to another and should take the lead in improvement of court procedures and practices. With the advice of a judicial council, he should be empowered to establish regulations requiring reasonable uniformity in the exercise of such judicial duties as sentencing.

The states should also adopt means additional to the impeachment process for removal of any judge not qualified for further service for physical, mental or other reasons.*

The impeachment process was intended to protect the independence of the judiciary against abuse of executive power, but experience at state-local levels reveals the need for disqualification procedures to deal with problems other than high crimes and misdemeanors—senility, alcoholism, permanent physical disability, and chronic absenteeism. California's Commission on Judicial Qualifications was established in 1960 to deal with such cases—usually through persuasion—and it has been copied in several other states.

Statistical information on state and local court operations is generally inadequate. Neither the public nor the state legislatures have the knowledge necessary to form reliable judgments on performance or the need for reforms. The U.S. Bureau of the Census has recently undertaken a survey of court structures, jurisdiction, and personnel in the 200 largest counties. This is a beginning; but annual collection and compilation of uniform and universal data on backlogs, case dispositions, and other matters is an obvious necessity.

Federal legislation should direct the Administrative Office of the United States Courts to collect appropriate data from all state and local courts.*

The key to effective action in all these areas is financial assistance; there is scant hope for speedy progress without this incentive.

Federal aid for state-local court systems should be conditioned upon acceptance and installation of the major reforms advocated in this chapter.

---

*See Memoranda by MR. ALEXANDER L. STOTT, page 76.

3.

STRENGTHENING COUNSEL IN CRIMINAL PROCEEDINGS

THIS COUNTRY accepts the principle that adversary proceedings are most likely to secure justice. Hence, there is concern for the quality of both prosecution and defense. Those accused have the right to legal counsel—at public expense for indigents—from arrest through every stage of those proceedings, but that right will be fully effective only when the scarcity of qualified defense counsel is overcome through better compensation, judicial insistence, and other determined efforts. Unjust treatment will then be less likely. But comparable measures to elevate the quality of prosecution are also needed and depend upon state and county actions that have not yet been taken.

The prosecutor has great discretion; the proper exercise of that discretion is essential to the ends of justice. Yet the experienced, non-political prosecutor is a rarity. Most often he is a locally elected official whose methods and philosophy are subject to little control or guidance —often varying drastically from those of other prosecutors exercising the same responsibilities under identical laws.

23

The burden of prosecution has grown to huge dimensions. There were over 1,500,000 arrests in 1970 for the seven Index crimes. The estimate for other arrests in addition to minor traffic offenses exceeded 6,500,000—including over 400,000 for drug violations and half a million for drunken driving. Charges are dropped in many of these cases, and one-third of the remainder are referred to juvenile courts. Still, the residual caseloads are unmanageable, often overwhelming.

Confronted with staggering caseloads, weak prosecuting units have been forced into an indefensible solution for their problems. A census found 56,000 arraigned persons held in local jails awaiting trial in 1969 and 27,000 not yet arraigned. Additional tens of thousands were out on bail. If all of these defendants were to insist upon formal trial, particularly trial by jury, the whole judicial system—encumbered by overloaded dockets and limited by court capacity—might well collapse. Hence, when there is much doubt of conviction, charges are often dropped. Even when there is strong evidence available, prosecutors commonly seek to "come into agreement" with defense counsel on a guilty plea by the defendant, usually for a lesser offense.

Pretrial discussions between prosecutor and defense counsel may be useful, particularly when youthful or first offenders are before the bar of justice, but plea bargaining undertaken *merely to mitigate intolerable congestion of court dockets* is a travesty on justice. Police and prosecutors should draft charges with care in the first instance, and when the evidence supports only a lesser charge, the change should be made without pressure upon the defendant to offer a guilty plea. The guilty ought not to be able to take advantage of congestion and the innocent should be assured of a fair trial. Agreements between prosecution and defense counsel should be subjected to intensive judicial scrutiny, and overturned when there is doubt that justice is well served.

Improper plea bargaining is often viewed as the only escape when the prosecution is starved for funds. State and local expenditures for this vital function in fiscal 1969 were miniscule in relation to caseloads, less than $40 for the average arrest. This compares with over $2,000 for the average criminal case commenced in the federal district courts that year. More was spent for indigent defense in the 35,000 federal cases than by all the states and local governments in dealing with their millions of arrests—$39.8 million *vs.* $37.9 million.

Prosecution is a top-level governmental function. It should not be subjected to control or starvation by the counties—which with a few exceptions are the most machine-ridden and poorly managed of local governments. Three-fourths of the counties are too small and too weak in resources to maintain a suitable prosecuting staff. Some have difficulty finding an attorney willing to run for election. Compensation is almost everywhere below levels attractive to qualified attorneys—either for elective posts or supporting staffs. Most elective prosecutors and many staff members serve only part-time (83 per cent of 1,000 responding to a 1965 survey), which leads to conflicts of interest and relative neglect of public duties.

Only three states (Alaska, Delaware, and Rhode Island) have state prosecution systems; two others (Connecticut and New Jersey) have state-appointed local prosecutors. All others elect prosecutors on a county or district basis, or both. In urban areas where municipal officers have some share in prosecution, further fragmentation results. State attorneys general seldom exercise more than sporadic supervision, even where they have constitutional authority to do so.

Prosecutors chosen by partisan ballot are usually nominated by and beholden to their party organizations. Many hope for political advancement and select staff members with partisan considerations in mind. The usual term of office is four years, in some states only two. Turnover of youthful and inexperienced aides is high, especially among the most able. There are outstanding examples of well-managed offices led by elected prosecutors of distinction, but they are rare.

Partisan politics also intrudes upon federal prosecutions, although to a lesser degree. United States Attorneys are Presidential appointees, free from the costs and risks of election. But Congressional pressures, together with political screenings by Attorneys General, make these appointments partisan, and recipients are expected to offer their resignations to an incoming President. Turnover is high here, also, in spite of better compensation.

We recognize, of course, that appointment of a director of prosecutions by a chief executive or an attorney general implies a broad policy or political relationship. This is as it should be. Philosophical views of politics and jurisprudence are germane to top appointments. But longer tenure would not be inconsistent with this concept. What is abhorrent is intrusion by low-level ward partisanship in this crucial function of government.

All state and local prosecuting staffs should be placed on a nonpartisan merit basis, with appropriate compensation and tenure; staffing patterns should conform with actual caseloads and backlogs; and all staffs should be fully funded.

25

Chief prosecutors and their staffs should serve on a full-time basis, without outside practice. This should apply immediately in urban areas and eventually everywhere. Subordinate staff should be placed under civil service rules wherever the state or local governments maintain civil service systems, but qualifications for appointment should include a broad educational background.

The United Kingdom provides sharp contrasts in its prosecutions. It has no elective judges or prosecutors, and no comparable prosecuting staffs. Either an injured party or a police officer may act as complainant. Except for the most serious crimes, cases are commonly tried without benefit of counsel. A barrister is employed *ad hoc* by the police or on behalf of the Crown only when counsel appears for the defense or when a felony is charged. The Director of Public Prosecutions has discretion to intervene in serious cases, and authority to see that barristers are employed or assigned to them. Judges have an active, aggressive role. Trial juries are small; grand juries are no longer used. While it is true that defendants enjoy fewer of the important rights and protections that they have in this country, they do obtain immediate trials and prompt verdicts.

Drastic revision of the American approach to prosecution was needed long before the onset of the present emergency; it has become imperative. The English example, based on a common law shared with this country, has attractive features. Speedy trial is assured, with no congested backlog. Narrow partisan politics does not intrude upon the administration of criminal justice. The need for high professional qualities of skill and integrity in prosecution is recognized. Most important of all, perhaps, prosecution is managed on a centralized basis.

Prosecution for violations of state laws should be centrally managed by each state. This would be consistent with the consolidation of state-local court systems proposed in this statement.

A State Director of Prosecutions should be appointed in each state by the Governor or the Attorney General, under a selection process that emphasizes merit. The Director should have full administrative authority, with power to establish and enforce standards for this function, and with the resources to provide and assign the professional staff necessary to supplement or substitute for prosecutors in every state (or local) court.

Outright and total statewide consolidation of this function, while ideal, will require amendment of many state constitutions. This is usually a lengthy process, but in most states an office of the kind here described could be created in the interim by statute and placed within the office of the Attorney General or directly under the Governor.

We recommend that heavy backlogs in urban centers or elsewhere be overcome at once through use of enough special prosecutors to assure "speedy and public" trials; that permanent staffs be expanded to the full extent of need; that chief prosecutors collaborate with court administrators to design improved scheduling arrangements; and that plea bargaining be subjected to close judicial scrutiny.

Both defense and prosecution should have full access to competent legal assistance. The shortage of attorneys serving the criminal courts on both sides leads to repeated court continuances that impede justice. The provision of special, *ad hoc* prosecutors would be an appropriate counterpart to the part-time volunteers who often serve as legal counsel to indigent defendants. Care must be taken, of course, to ensure maintenance of quality standards in all these proceedings.

Those states still requiring indictments to be returned only by grand juries should eliminate that rule. Grand juries should focus attention upon special situations, such as those involving official corruption.

Many of the 50 states have eliminated the rigid requirement that grand juries must hand down all indictments for serious offenses. There is a growing consensus that this is archaic. Grand juries place heavy burdens on the prosecution and create long delays in resolution of criminal charges. The composition of grand jury panels is also subject to challenge. States now using other arrangements show no signs of return to the former practice, nor of any resulting denial of substantive justice. Professional, tenured, and properly supervised prosecution would make the rigid grand jury requirement obsolete. Prosecutors could then be trusted to bring cases before the courts without delay, upon presentment of information.

Every thorough study of prosecution in this country, from the Wickersham Commission onward, has deplored prevailing conditions and urged a stronger role for the states. But suggested remedies have usually been too restrained—through concern for long tradition, the political influence of local prosecutors, and the barriers imposed by state constitutions. If this country intends to deal seriously with its crime problem, such timidity must be overcome.

Much will depend upon the legal profession, which now shows increasing interest in criminal law. Compressed into a single, uninspiring course, criminal law was long the stepchild of the nation's law schools. The field has been unattractive in terms of remuneration; it had also

27

fallen into public disrepute. Its intellectual content is being broadened by sociological and constitutional additions, but law schools still focus on textbook cases, particularly appellate cases and legal doctrines—without adequate attention to the structure of the criminal justice system, as dealt with in this report. In the past, few top law graduates entered the practice of criminal law.

This condition is not in the national interest, since establishing order with justice should engage highly qualified legal talent. There are some signs of change, however. A movement toward off-campus clinical experience in courtrooms and law offices, chiefly concerned with defense and other legal services to the indigent, is sweeping through the law schools. This clinical experience can provide a linkage between legal doctrine and the need for improvement throughout the whole field of criminal justice, exciting the interest of outstanding students.

Educators and lawyers should intensify their efforts to elevate the practice of criminal law to a position of higher respect in the legal community. Law students should be exposed to administration of justice problems outside the courtroom—to the operative legal system as well as legal doctrine. They should have direct clinical experience, also, under capable supervision, in dealing with men and women in actual cases.

In every aspect of prosecution, as in judicial proceedings, a new and serious concern for effective administration should command a very high priority.

4.

MODERNIZING THE POLICE

POLICE RESPONSIBILITIES include the preservation of public order, protection of persons and property, and crime prevention—as well as detection and apprehension of offenders. Roles vary accordingly, from the semimilitary posture required in handling unruly crowds to those of street patrolman, traffic controller, defender against armed violators, protector of the neglected child, diplomatic intervenor in family or neighborhood quarrels, investigator using advanced scientific methods, or manager of a large-scale diversified organization. Attitudes and training required for such varied duties also differ, to the point of inconsistency.

The special importance of the police rests on the fact that they are the most visible symbols of governmental authority. They deal directly with people on a day-to-day and face-to-face basis; the impact of their broad, on-the-spot discretion ought not to be underestimated. Minor offenses may be dealt with or ignored; offenders may be arrested or merely admonished; neighborhood melees may be quieted tactfully or escalated into major disturbances; and group animosities may be minimized or exacerbated. Personal and professional qualifications of the police are crucial, then, in building mutual support between officers of the law and the community.

Threatened by dangerous disorders and rising crime rates, the public's first response is to call for more money for more police. Both money and manpower have been provided in large measure; police employment rose 38 per cent from 1962 to 1970. However, crimes reported to the police increased by 150 per cent over those years. Citizens have been slow to see that without able prosecution, speedy trials, and suitable correctional measures the police cannot restrain crime successfully. Nor is it fully understood, in view of the variety and complexity of the work, that reorganization and better management are often as important to a modern force as additional policemen.

In fact, police forces are not so badly undermanned or underfunded as other elements of the criminal justice system. Nationwide, police number over 500,000, averaging one for every 400 inhabitants. Their annual payrolls neared $4 billion in 1969, rising well above $5 billion in 1971—over half of all criminal justice expenditures. But major difficulties, such as structural fragmentation and ineffective internal management, are unresolved. Reciprocal antipathies between police and some segments of the population are discussed in chapter 7. Corruption—a most serious problem—is dealt with in chapter 6.

Here again, as with courts and prosecutions, the states have primary responsibility. Local forces derive their authority from the states, which have done little to elevate police standards or to overcome major deficiencies. At the same time, the distribution of federal funds newly available for improvement of police and other criminal justice functions has been poorly managed by the states, through planning mechanisms that have proved seriously inadequate.

FRAGMENTATION OF POLICE FORCES is extreme; there are 32,000 separate police departments. New York City has 37,500 police employees, while thousands of small municipalities have only one part-time officer. Some 3,000 county sheriffs are elected by partisan ballot, with authority overlapping other jurisdictions; their forces range from 6,500 in Los Angeles County down to one in many cases. Most townships have constables, and some special districts have police. All states except Hawaii have their own forces (or highway patrols), with a combined strength of 55,000. The national government has four specialized law enforcement units which, along with the FBI, numbered 36,000 in 1970.

Wasted energies and lost motion due to overlapping, duplication, and noncooperation are not the worst consequences of this fragmentation. Large areas of the United States—particularly rural communities and the small jurisdictions in or near metropolitan areas—lack anything resembling modern, professional police protection. But ease of travel and communication is breaking down the isolation of such areas; their crime rates are rising faster than those of the cities. Their forces are under-equipped and unprepared by serious training even for standard assignments; organized crime and the narcotics traffic are beyond their reach.

State police forces have not cured the deficiency. Barely half have statewide investigative authority; only seven carry a full range of police responsibility. Everywhere, they are thinly spread and mainly oriented to highway patrol. This preoccupation leaves most of them without the means—even where they have legal authority—to provide investigative or other support for weak local forces. Immediate expansion and reorientation of state forces is the least that the legislatures could provide.

Substitution of strong statewide or regionally organized police forces for small, ineffective local units should have immediate consideration. The state police should provide assistance in training, and offer specialized central staff services for larger local forces. They could supersede small, untrained local forces in dealing with felonies. Township constables, deputy sheriffs, and village marshals could then concentrate upon local violations and service functions.

State forces should be expected to cope with criminal syndicates, and meet other challenges to the public safety. The syndicates have proven their ability to gain outright control over some local governments. Conditions in metropolitan areas facilitate such efforts; in the 30 with populations over one million, there were 1,403 separate local police forces in 1967. Half of these had 20 or fewer employees. Inefficiency and lack of coordination are regrettable, but fragmentation also creates havens for illicit operations—weakening every aspect of police protection.

State police forces should be expanded and strengthened to assure proper protection for the entire population, especially in areas without effective local forces.

But grouping police in fewer and larger forces is only a partial solution. Half of the nation's most serious crimes occur under the jurisdiction of the 66 largest local forces (55 city and 11 county), although only one-fourth of the population is protected by them. Each of these forces has over 500 employees, but mere size has not given

31

them an ability to meet the challenge of increasing crime. Consolidations should go forward, but other changes are also essential.

POLICE MANAGEMENT is undergoing closer scrutiny, partly because of the low ratio of serious crimes solved, or "cleared by arrest." In cities over 250,000 in 1970 only 30 per cent of all robberies, 22 per cent of all burglaries, 13 per cent of all larcenies over $50, and 17 per cent of all auto thefts known to the police were "cleared" by an arrest. The precise accuracy of these data may be questioned; the fact that most such crimes are never solved is not in doubt. The nationwide "clearance rate" for all seven Index offenses fell from 31 per cent in 1960 to 20 per cent in 1970. Nearly half of those arrested were juveniles—relatively easy to apprehend. Of the 54 per cent who were adults, barely half were found guilty as charged. Attention must be directed, therefore, toward the competence of police management.

Police management is an exacting assignment. Yet few chiefs of police, or their deputies and assistants, have had in-depth training or preparation designed to develop managerial skills. Promotions in city forces are usually made from within, limiting top jobs to those recruited as patrolmen 20 or 30 years ago when physical factors were more heavily stressed than educational preparation or basic mental capacity. In the counties elective sheriffs and their deputies are chosen for their political, and not their managerial qualifications. Police forces do contain many men of high intelligence, vigor, and integrity, but few who are prepared to question traditional structures or obsolescent attitudes.

Transfers of professionally trained officers between police forces are still rare except at the highest levels. State and local laws and regulations limit pension eligibility to officers who serve 20 years or more within a single jurisdiction. Accumulated benefits are lost by those who accept promotional transfers; rights are not vested. Some distinguished police chiefs, after serving three or four cities in the course of 30-year careers, have no pension prospects whatever. Reluctantly, since other means seem unavailable, we are led to conclude that federal action is needed to overcome this barrier, through direct funding or pressure on the states.

Police management must be greatly strengthened through: (a) insistence upon high professional qualifications for all upper-level appointments; (b) attraction through lateral entry of technical specialists from outside and skilled officers from other well-managed forces; (c) establishment of a nationwide pension system for qualified professionals,

32

to encourage such transfers; (d) intensive, continuous management training for all supervisory ranks; (e) reduction in the average number of persons reporting to each responsible officer; (f) provision of central staff for top police management adequate in number and competence for planning, personnel, and investigative purposes; and (g) frequent evaluations of police performance by objective external agencies, such as the International Association of Chiefs of Police or management consulting firms using clearly defined national criteria.

The need for strong professional management is obvious in view of technological developments, organizational complexities, obstacles to optimal utilization of available manpower, and difficulties arising from animosities between police and the populations served. The qualities of leadership and the management skills required are of high order. Resistance to change is deeply imbedded, but reorganizations already achieved or in progress show that obstacles are not insuperable.

Every large force assigns a significant share of its manpower to supportive functions such as communications, records, property and equipment management, personnel management, and laboratory work. These call for specialized competencies unrelated to the usual range of police work. They do not involve face-to-face contacts with the public, for which patrolmen should be well prepared. Such activities should not be manned by uniformed officers whose skills are badly needed elsewhere and whose pay levels exceed prevailing scales for comparable jobs in the local labor market. The International Association of Chiefs of Police regards a proportion of *at least* 20 per cent civilians in police departments as optimal. Not many forces meet that standard.

Management of motor vehicular traffic is a major governmental concern, but its effective execution depends more on engineering, architectural, planning, and computer skills than upon police patrols. Personnel specializing in traffic direction and parking controls could function well under organizational leadership separated from other police responsibilities. Traffic courts and insurance regulation are closely related to this field of management.

Prompt response to pleas for help or reports of suspicious actions has high priority, but police resources for such purposes are reduced by: (a) diversion of well-trained patrolmen to report parking and other minor vehicular violations or to provide routine direction of traffic flows, along with resulting court appearances; and (b) the drain from excessive numbers of precinct stations in large cities, staffed around-the-clock with manpower trained primarily for other duties.

Police administrators seldom deploy enough well-qualified people to concentrate on the suppression of serious crimes, narcotics abuse, or organized crime—which are quite rightly major concerns of the public. Those assigned are from the ranks; special units charged with such responsibilities contain few if any members of the standard professions —attorneys, statisticians, accountants, engineers, psychologists, computer specialists, and the like. These must be brought in, if at all, through lateral entry and paid above beginning police scales. Each major force should have a strong investigative unit manned by highly skilled and well-paid specialists.

Patrol forces, on foot or motorized, should be strengthened and given special training; diversion to other duties should be minimized. The training and indoctrination needed by patrol officers has little relevance to internal support assignments involving records, communications, laboratories, or property management. Such training is used below capacity in traffic direction and on parking violations, but is inadequate for investigative duties involving the most serious crimes. Large forces may set up separate divisions of community service officers, another field calling for careful preparation. Top management should have flexibility in its control over all assignments.

The different kinds of work done by police forces large enough to allow a degree of specialization should be fully recognized organizationally as well as in recruitment and training. Pay scales for supportive and other nonuniformed activities should conform with those prevailing in the civilian labor market.

The collective or conspiratorial crimes of organized syndicates create a special problem. These depredations depend upon webs of covert agreements and understandings not readily brought to light by ordinary police operations. The initial successes of "strike forces" mobilized against the syndicates in a score of large cities by the U.S. Department of Justice, staffed with highly qualified and diversified personnel drawn from several agencies, are encouraging.

The "strike force" approach pioneered by the Department of Justice in efforts to suppress organized crime should be strengthened and expanded; state police forces and those of major cities might well establish similar units wherever the syndicates have taken root.

These measures, together with those discussed in chapters 6 and 7, afford hope for success against the insidious operations of organized criminal groups.

34

Over eight million young Americans are presently enrolled in colleges and universities. Many should be brought into police work and other phases of law enforcement as cadets, either part- or full-time; graduates should be encouraged to take up such careers. The graduates of those few universities such as Michigan State that provide four-year curricula in police administration have brought a professional outlook into the forces employing them.

Cooperative arrangements between police departments and educational institutions benefit both, and should be strongly encouraged. Monroe Community College in Rochester, New York, offers a two-year associate degree program in police science. Graduates are employed by the local police department as trainees, even before they reach the minimum age for appointment as officers. Comparable arrangements can and should be widely extended.

Few police officers have had much exposure to the systematic study of management, and administrative experience is generally limited to a single jurisdiction. Serious attention should be given to creation of a curriculum in police administration—which could be expanded to cover all aspects of criminal justice—in a national collegiate center. Establishment of a national college of police administration has been strongly urged, to emphasize and improve opportunities for professional management. It could also stress research, utilizing other university and private agency resources as well as its own. This concept, which is designed to broaden educational backgrounds and strengthen management skills in police administration, should be extended to include personnel concerned with the entire range of criminal justice activities. This project is worthy of thorough exploration.

Police departments should establish cooperative arrangements with colleges and universities, both for police cadets at recruitment levels and for higher ranks seeking professional development.

Officers should be thoroughly familiar with the rudiments of criminal law and procedure, particularly as these apply to arrests, searches, and seizures. Careful training in the rules of evidence would assist in obtaining convictions and would lessen the chances that legal technicalities may thwart justice. Professionalism must extend to the lower as well as the higher ranks, as is recognized by several West Coast cities.

Police officers should have ready access to advisory legal counsel, either under departmental auspices or through close liaison with prosecution staffs.

35

Management must inculcate professional standards governing all police dealings with minorities through: (a) careful screening in the selection process; (b) intensive sensitivity training; (c) immediate and impartial investigation of all allegations of police misconduct, followed by appropriate action; and (d) continuous supervisory leadership. Police work is no career for persons unable to subordinate prejudice; unless assignments without public contacts can be found for them they must be dropped. Intensive supervision in this and other vital matters (including temptations to corruption) during a probationary period of one year and thereafter is essential. This implies the need for enough officers of middle grade to maintain active supervision over the lower ranks.

Recruiting efforts among all population groups not represented proportionately on police forces must be deliberately intensified. This applies to employment of women, which is increasing as it should. If qualifications on height and formal education have to be waived—pending successful probation—then they should. State and national police forces with high professional and compensation standards are among the worst in this regard, with token or no representation for even the largest of minorities. Since these forces tend to set the tone for the whole law enforcement establishment, they must take strong corrective action to preserve their high status.

Discriminatory treatment cannot be tolerated. At stake is citizen confidence that protection and assistance are the primary police objectives. Observance of common courtesy and friendly bearing toward the public will help to generate community rapport. It must be made clear that use of excessive force by police officers constitutes unprofessional conduct punishable by appropriate disciplinary action extending to dismissal.

Heavy stress should be placed upon police attitudes and standards of conduct in dealing with the public—through recruitment policies, training, and performance evaluation.[1]

Accusations of police misconduct are frequently heard and widely believed in many American communities. Such beliefs pose a grave danger, since lawless conduct on the part of the police surely encourages the breakdown of social order. This concern is not without substance. In a 1966 study of police conduct 36 observers accom-

---

[1] The conflicts inherent in the role and identity of the police in an urban society are dealt with in CED's latest Supplementary Paper: Robert F. Steadman, editor, *The Police and the Community* (Baltimore: The Johns Hopkins University Press, 1972).

panied police on duty, reporting 5,360 occasions when 597 policemen dealt with 11,255 citizens in Boston, Chicago, and Washington, D.C.[2] Although the officers knew that records of their behavior were being kept, one out of five "was observed in criminal violation of the law"— over and above contacts with organized crime and illegal assaults on citizens.

The violations reported included theft of merchandise from establishments after burglaries, taking money and property from sex deviants, accepting money to alter sworn testimony, taking bribes not to issue traffic tickets, and accepting money or goods from merchants. Forty per cent of the officers also violated important departmental regulations at least once. In 10 per cent of the contacts, police used an authoritarian manner or subjected citizens to ridicule; excessive force was reported in three of every 1,000 contacts. At the same time, in 43 per cent of all situations where the observers judged that felonious offenses had been observed, no arrest was made. Only professionals of high caliber under constant supervision should be entrusted with the broad discretion exercised routinely by police officers.

More than strong management is needed to ensure professional police conduct. In this country no private citizen can initiate a criminal proceeding in court, no matter how deeply aggrieved he or she may be. Criminal charges have to be brought through official channels, by the police, or prosecutors, or grand juries—making it hard to bring police officers to account for unlawful actions. Higher authorities tend to disbelieve or disregard allegations of this nature, while prosecutors and grand juries often condone police excesses. The practice differs fundamentally in England; there, any citizen may bring a criminal action against a police officer directly into court, placing police conduct under direct judicial surveillance.

Criminal charges against police officers (as well as prison guards and other officers of the law) should be prosecuted as such, and private parties should be enabled to bring such cases before the courts.

Pouring money into the police function at all levels, without making some fundamental adjustments, is unlikely to produce the desired results. The changes we propose do not require constitutional amendments; legislative and administrative action by the states and the national government would suffice.

---

[2] See Albert J. Reiss, Jr., *The Police and the Public* (New Haven: Yale University Press, 1971).

Financial aid by federal (and state) governments to local forces ought to be conditioned upon acceptance and maintenance of reasonable standards. Moreover, such aid should be limited to forces large enough to function effectively in the modern environment, with jurisdiction over areas and populations sufficient to support the full range of police responsibilities.

The waste and misuse of public funds evident in the conduct of grant programs under the Law Enforcement Assistance Administration (LEAA) of the Department of Justice should be brought to an end. Federal funds should be used to raise standards, not to subsidize ineffective local operations.

5.

REFORMING CORRECTIONS

ALLOUS NEGLECT has produced a debacle of major proportions in the nation's misguided and under-funded correctional efforts. (There are 1,600,000 convicts under current correctional controls, ranging in degree from occasional supervisory interviews to penal measures of great severity.) The curative quality of these efforts is so ineffective that society continues to suffer from subsequent violations by these same individuals. (Most juvenile offenders are placed on probation, with little supervision or aid in solving their problems.) For the most part, prisons are full of older, hardened products of failure to change patterns of juvenile delinquency. The impersonal, mass approach to corrections dominates—although the one best hope rests on personal, individual attention to each offender.

Public opinion has arrived at no consensus concerning the basic purposes of corrections. One view holds that fear of punishment will deter unlawful conduct. Another sees rehabilitation as the main objective, convinced that attitudes may be changed through stimulation of new motivations and provision of employable skills. But the prevalence of crime proves that deterrence is not wholly effective—whether because punishment is not severe enough or not certain enough or because the concept is faulty. And high rates of recidivism (relapse into criminal activity) show that traditional rehabilitative efforts have failed; prisons and reformatories appear to reinforce criminal inclinations.

The issue cannot be put aside; the number of habitual criminals is growing too rapidly to permit further evasion. If attitudes, addictions, and patterns of conduct found among first or minor offenders go uncorrected, then life-long criminal careers entailing enormous social and economic damage will follow. Criminal behavior, like all human behavior, is characteristically repetitive.

The entire correctional system is failing and in need of drastic reconstruction. Intensive research may yield clearer directions over the long run, but pending such results pragmatism would dictate this guiding principle: **rehabilitative effort should be maximized in every aspect of the correctional apparatus, while the loss of personal freedom should be used as a deterrent only under constructive conditions emphasizing ordinary human decency and avoiding punitive degradation.**

The size and scope of the problem have been concealed by its dispersion among national, state, and local authorities and by lack of comprehensive statistics. Recent studies show, however, that nearly 2 per cent of all males over the age of 12 are currently under correctional restraint. About 900,000 persons are under probationary supervision; 300,000 are in prisons plus 54,000 in juvenile detention facilities; and 300,000 are on parole after release from confinement. Still another 75,000 are in jails awaiting trial, not technically under correctional control because theoretically innocent until proven guilty—a distinction often blurred in practice.

Unacceptable conditions mark every aspect of the correctional effort: in pretrial detention, in sentencing procedures, in probationary supervision, in jails and prisons, and in parole. Governmental apathy is appalling; correctional expenditures are less than one-third those for "police protection"—while the police are called on to arrest over and over persons whose patterns of conduct have been worsened, not bettered, by "corrections."

PRETRIAL DETENTION of those unable to obtain bail, and not released on their own recognizance or to specific custody, is largely the responsibility of 4,000 local jails. These also house persons convicted of minor offenses, with short sentences. Prisoners are held for months or years awaiting trial; convictions often lead to prison sentences shorter than the time already spent in jail. Meanwhile, the innocent and first offenders are thrown together with habitual criminals and frequently subjected to sexual assault. Speedy trials and a lesser role for grand juries would sharply reduce jail populations. So would greater restraint by judges in requiring bail, and the abolition of bail bond profiteering.

Many of these jails are old, below acceptable physical standards. Worse, they lack recreational, educational, or medical facilities. Many are too small to be efficient; others, although large, are extremely overcrowded. Jailers and guards are rarely qualified. The corrective or curative element in these jails is nonexistent, but their ability to foster antisocial attitudes and to function as schools for crime is well documented.

Constitutionally, persons charged with crime are presumed innocent until tried and found guilty, and should be treated accordingly. Where court appearance may reasonably be expected, the accused should be released, pending trial. Bail bond rackets should be suppressed.

Local jails should be required to meet standards consistent with the presumption of innocence. Juveniles should not be housed with convicted criminals nor with adults awaiting trial. The states should relieve local units of all responsibility for imprisonment of those convicted, and this would be preferred for pretrial detentions as well. Connecticut, Delaware, and Rhode Island have assumed full state responsibility for detention. They have no local jails, an example deserving emulation.

SENTENCES imposed on conviction are highly variable, ranging for the same crime between extremes in leniency and severity not only from state to state but from judge to judge within the same court system. Two felons convicted of identical offenses and with comparable case histories may receive prison terms differing in length by three or four to one, and most court systems lack means to minimize such discrepancies. Judges have little guidance by statute or education on sentencing philosophy or alternatives; many even lack personal knowledge of prison conditions. Judicial conferences, seminars, and summer sessions on such subjects hold promise and should be more widely used. Pre-sentence investigation—proven to be a very valuable tool—is commonly sketchy or nonexistent. Many prisoners begin their terms embittered by the sincere belief that they have been sentenced capriciously and hence unjustly.

Greater consistency should be applied in sentencing persons convicted of the same crimes, within each consolidated state judiciary (and within the federal judiciary as well), through insistent pressure from the chief justice, the judicial council, or both. Trial juries should not determine sentences.

Judges should have every means to obtain all pre-sentence information needed in each case. Under federal practice the choice of prison is made by the corrections authority following careful individual study —after sentence has been set—and *not* by the trial judge. The states might well follow this lead. Moreover, much closer attention should be given to restitution, or money damages to the victims of crime, in lieu of prison sentences.

PROBATION under suspended sentence is a far more frequent penalty than a prison or reformatory term, particularly for juveniles and first offenders. (Probationers outnumber prison inmates by three to one.) The number is rising as crime rates rise, whereas prison populations are actually declining. These diverse trends stem from two causes: the increasing disrepute of American prisons, and the relatively low public expenditure required for each probationer (only $250 in 1965). Judges aware of actual prison conditions prefer to avoid commitments, and the public is repelled by frequent scandals and riots. Moreover, probation has more to be said for it than low cost; most criminologists agree that when properly administered it holds greater prospect of rehabilitation than imprisonment does under prevailing conditions.[1]

(Probation is less successful than could be expected if it were better managed.) Supervision is usually prescribed, implying frequent contacts with qualified probation officers. But probation staffs are undermanned, undertrained, and underpaid. The standard maximum of 35 probationers for each probation officer seems moderate; it may be too high.[2] Yet, in 1965, 77 per cent of all officers dealing with juveniles had caseloads over 60; only 4 per cent had 40 or less. Their role is critical; if properly executed fewer than the present quarter of all paroles might lead to revocation for violations. Increasing millions of

---

[1] See, for example, Karl Menninger, *The Crime of Punishment* (New York: Viking Press, 1968).

[2] See U.S. President's Commission on Law Enforcement and the Administration of Justice, *Task Force Report: Corrections* (1967).

42

American children are neglected; the neglected child is quite likely to become delinquent. Then the community, through the probation officer, must act *in loco parentis*. Failure here is ruinous to the child and costly to society.

Two-thirds of all officers concerned with adult offenders had caseloads over 100; only one per cent had 40 or less. In 1931, the Wickersham Commission stressed the need for adequate numbers of highly qualified and well-trained probation officers, but the deficiency continues. Doubling or trebling the number of officers, providing more training and better pay, and expanding counseled employment for probationers would still leave costs far below those for imprisonment. These steps would be less expensive than a 10 per cent pay increase for all police forces, and the probability of positive results would be high. Experiments with well-trained citizen volunteers accepting one-to-one supervisory roles, and with use of case aides who live in the same neighborhoods as those on parole, hold considerable promise but do not minimize the need for strong professional leadership.

PAROLE standards assume grave importance also. Parolees number 300,000 and there are growing pressures to expand parole opportunities. Parole presents harder problems than probation; most parolees have longer histories of more serious criminal conduct than probationers. Furthermore, the difficulties faced by ex-prisoners branded as convicts while trying to establish "normal" modes of employment, family and social life are quite forbidding in the light of prevailing community attitudes.

Assistance in this transition calls for unusual skill and competence. The stigma attached to "ex-convicts" in American society is a heavy handicap in finding or holding suitable employment and in assuming a constructive life style. On-the-job success would go far to prevent recidivism; the business community has a responsibility here that is not being well met. Moreover, in parole as in probation, caseloads are excessive. In 1965, 92 per cent of parole officers dealing with adults had more than 50 convicts in charge, as did 72 per cent of those in charge of juvenile parolees. Such caseloads only *seem* inexpensive. There is an imperative need for clearer standards, both in granting and administering parole, and for individual guidance to parolees.

Probationary and parole forces must be strongly reinforced, reoriented, and reorganized; they are society's main resource in diverting offenders, whether juvenile or adult, occasional or habitual, minor or

43

major, from continuance in criminal courses of conduct. The business community should work closely with these forces in providing job opportunities, and otherwise.

This clearly implies doubling—or trebling—the number of probation and parole officers, increasing compensation, elevating admissions and in-training requirements to a professional level, setting and insisting upon observance of high standards, and providing supervisory leadership of a high order. It may well be that the desired results can be achieved only by making both probation and parole primarily state (and federal) functions, with chief executives held fully responsible for effective performance. The supplementary cooperation of trained civilian volunteers for one-to-one work with both probationers and parolees is an objective to be vigorously pursued.

PRISONS are viewed by many as the key factor in corrections. In one sense this is accurate; most inmates have been convicted of serious offenses or have had several convictions, and prisons account for the bulk of all correctional expenditures. But their importance in prevention or control of criminality is doubtful at best. Most inmates are not committed until patterns of criminal conduct are already firmly established; 93 per cent are 20 years of age or older. Most remain for relatively brief periods of time, but are repeatedly recommitted.

Theoretically, rehabilitation is a primary objective of imprisonment, but in practice it is subordinated to the intended deterrent effects of tight custody, regimentation, and a climate of repression. The "good prisoner" is one who seems subdued in that environment—a disqualification for successful post-release adjustment. Prison systems range in quality from marginal acceptability in those of a few states and the federal government, down to the medieval level of some state and local systems. Facilities are severely overcrowded and generally below acceptable physical standards; narcotics traffic and sexual abuses thrive.

The failure rate is very high; 63 per cent of federal parolees released in 1963 were rearrested within six years, as were 76 per cent of those given mandatory releases. Such information as is available indicates that experience with state prison releases is comparable. The appalling fact is that firm statistical data on recidivism is practically nonexistent at state-local levels. Only occasional spot studies have been made and coordination of records from the many state, local, and federal institutions has not been attempted. This is needed to permit systematic evaluation results from each element in the correctional system.

44

Rehabilitative efforts vary, but few teachers, psychologists or psychiatrists are found on prison staffs. Many inmates have no work assignments; idleness is the chief prison occupation. Custodial restraints then breed resentment. The work that is available rarely fosters skills useful after discharge. Experience in producing license plates has slight value in the outside labor market.

Every objective study of American prisons has called attention to the low qualifications of prison guards, and to their lack of intensive training. Both the nature of their work and compensation scales are unattractive. The usual disciplinary emphasis encourages brutalization, greatly worsened where guards collude in the drug traffic or overlook inmate violence extending to homosexual assaults. Lives of prisoners are endangered by racial violence and other forms of internecine hostility. In many prisons, moreover, tensions between all-white staffs and prison populations dominated by militant blacks have reached explosive levels. Prisoners usually lack avenues of complaint and are denied access to legal counsel or other protections of due process; they are made to feel subhuman.

Many citizens take comfort from the high walls, watchtowers, and machine guns designed to forestall jailbreaks and to control increasingly frequent and deadly prison riots. They seem to feel that violence confined within prison walls is of no concern to them. But the effect of dehumanization upon 400 ex-prisoners released daily into the open society should be recognized. Nearly half of those in federal and state prisons on January 1, 1967 were released by the end of that year. Ex-prisoners out on parole outnumber the inmates inside. Prison riots are visible proof that presumed objectives are not being attained.

The courts have now begun to insist upon prison reforms. A federal district court has ordered sweeping changes in the conduct of Virginia's prisons; a state court in Maryland threatens to close one of its largest institutions unless rehabilitative emphasis is intensified; and Arkansas prisons are under court examination.

It is past time to give thoughtful reconsideration to the whole field of crime and punishment. The immediate necessity is to replace obsolete prisons, oppressively managed, with decent facilities where opportunities for education, training, and personal development are available under the guidance of qualified and sensitive staffs. No prison should be designed for more than 500 inmates, nor should any be allowed to accept prisoners in excess of rated capacity. Prisons should be located close to areas of family residence to allow easy visitation, and situated where there is access to varied outside employment for those on daily furloughs.

The cost of these changes will be considerable—perhaps $20,000 or more per inmate in construction alone, if educational, recreational, and training facilities are included. Still larger sums will be needed to provide curative facilities for alcoholism and drug addiction. All this must be placed in proper perspective, and compared with the costs borne by society because of the tens of thousands of hardened and embittered career criminals among the 100,000 to 150,000 released from American prisons each year. Cost effectiveness coincides with humanity in support of reform.

The state and national governments must provide smaller, uncrowded, properly located prison facilities—with suitable living space, training equipment, and staff support—to house those whose freedom is deemed so dangerous to society that it must be denied. Impartial inspection teams should make frequent visits to all prisons.

Many existing state prisons should be abandoned, or thoroughly redesigned and reconstructed. More space may be needed, particularly after all prisoners held in local jails are shifted to state institutions, but prisons (and work camps) should be far more specialized than most are—as to types of offenders, security requirements, and educational-vocational opportunities. Managements should foster better communications with inmates, through representative councils. Experiments with work release assignments, furloughs, halfway houses, and other forms of community-based corrections should be actively pursued.

At the same time, recent disuse and probable eventual abandonment of the death penalty lead toward lifelong incarceration without much hope of parole for those considered so dangerous to society that they must be held under maximum security.* Construction and equipment of appropriate facilities will cost money, as will the professional personnel of types and numbers needed, but interchange of prisoners between the states—and by them with the federal prison system—would lessen the costs of the proposed specialization.

CONSTRUCTIVE, IMAGINATIVE INITIATIVES for improvement of correctional methods have been undertaken here and there. These are worthy of special notice; they deserve thorough ex-

---

*See Memorandum by MR. DONALD S. PERKINS on page 76.

46

ploration, experimental application, and swift expansion wherever found to be successful.

■ Some jurisdictions are reducing numbers held in jail pending trial, by reforming bail procedures and shortening court delays, as pioneered by the City of Oakland, California, and the Vera Institute of Justice in New York City.

■ Better counseling and testing services are being developed in some places, especially for juveniles during the prehearing period, as in California.

■ Pre-sentence evaluations, psychological and social, hold great promise and are coming into wider use, as in Kansas and California.

■ There is an increasing trend toward measures to review sentences and bring them into closer uniformity, as in Connecticut, Maine, Maryland, and Massachusetts.

■ A few communities, such as Denver, Colorado, have enlisted and trained citizen volunteers willing to accept personal responsibility for maintenance of close supervisory contact with *one* individual probationer or parolee.

■ The U.S. District Court for the Northern District of Illinois is experimenting successfully with the use of neighborhood residents as case aides for probation and parole.

■ The State of California has developed a strong educational and training emphasis in its institutions for youthful offenders, followed by unusually strong support to parolees; Alabama, Oregon, and Wisconsin stress educational opportunities.

■ Work assignments stressing self-discipline more than close supervision for groups outside prison walls, in forests or elsewhere, have been successfully developed by the federal and some state penal systems.

■ Other prisons have begun to release inmates during daylight hours for outside jobs, as in North Carolina.

■ Furloughs for brief home visits are rewards for good conduct, as in the federal prison system, Mississippi and Michigan, with only one per cent return failure.

■ Some 200 halfway houses have been set up, where prisoners still under surveillance can live while readjusting to civilian life.

■ Minnesota has installed a system of "performance programming agreements"—signed by both the prisoner and the parole board—identifying the specific goals to be met by each prisoner before parole can be expected and assuring parole after fulfillment, assuming reasonably good behavior. This procedure is designed to reduce the caprice and bitterness generally associated with parole procedures.

■ Fines based on the difference between earnings and subsistence necessities for a stated period are imposed in preference to imprisonment, as in Sweden.

■ An ombudsman, appointed by and reporting directly to the Governor, has been established in Minnesota, to hear complaints and observe conditions concerning all prisons, juvenile institutions, and state probation and parole officers.

* * * *

State governments bear primary responsibility for the abuses and inadequacies found in the corrections system today. They must now provide the moral leadership and financial support for substantial change. Federal funds have been made available through the Law Enforcement Assistance Administration for all phases of crime reduction. Through 1971 few of these dollars were channeled toward corrections and least of all toward rehabilitation research, although future prospects have improved. Larger appropriations will be needed to build satisfactory correctional systems, and the states should not wait upon federal aids—beneficial though these would be. What the states do in this field will greatly affect the position they will hold in the American federal system of the future.

6.

ORGANIZED GAMBLING
AND OFFICIAL CORRUPTION

CRIME SYNDICATES have grown rich and powerful in this country by fulfilling the desire of significant numbers of people for illicit services or products. They gathered strength by helping citizens defy the prohibition of alcoholic beverages. After repeal they turned to comparable fields: notably gambling and, to a lesser extent, prostitution. More recently, they have moved into the growing traffic in narcotics and dangerous drugs. Success in any such operation depends greatly upon the collusion of persons engaged in law enforcement, which is frequently obtainable. It depends, also, on widespread willingness to flout laws that define as crimes violations of a moral code not generally accepted. Reluctance to modify criminal codes to conform with common social behavior thus bulwarks the syndicates in their conspiracies.

The resulting situation calls for modernization of the criminal codes on many fronts, as outlined in chapter 7. But the importance of gambling justifies separate, more extensive treatment. *Gambling is at the same time both the main source of illicit revenue for organized criminal syndicates and the primary channel to corruption of police and*

49

other officials. Organized crime cannot be controlled unless this enormous financial resource is cut off. Moreover, faith in the basic integrity of American justice cannot be restored without elimination of the official corruption fostered by illicit gambling.

Estimates by responsible sources place the gross annual illegal revenue from gambling (chiefly on races, athletic contests, and "the numbers") at from $20 billion to $50 billion, with the net to organized operatives at about one-third of the gross.[1] It is estimated that half of all television football fans make token bets, and that as much as 90 per cent of bookmakers' business stems from team sports.[2] For obvious reasons, winnings are seldom taxed.

Conclusive proof of official collusion in these far-flung activities is not easily established, but two propositions are axiomatic: first, that organized gambling on a significant scale cannot be carried on for long without the knowledge of the local police; and second, that such gambling is a fact of life in most if not all large cities.

Without the funds and organizational strength obtained through illicit gambling, syndicate members would be much less able to exploit other opportunities. It takes money, manpower, and often official protection to carry on profitable loan-sharking, labor racketeering, deliberate bankruptcies, counterfeiting, prostitution, traffic in narcotics, hijacking, fencing of stolen merchandise, and disposition of purloined securities through foreign and domestic channels. Without gambling revenues, it would be far more difficult to gain substantial footholds in legitimate enterprises

Efforts to legalize gambling are opposed by an unusual coalition of those horrified by official approval for gambling, and the powerfully entrenched underworld syndicates. Further opposition to legalization comes from police and other officials—some holding a sincere belief that there are other ways to suppress organized gambling, and some having a collusive interest in the proceeds. This diverse combination of forces has been quite successful, until recently, in resisting change.

This situation presents a number of perplexing issues. State laws prohibiting all gambling were originally adopted in conformity with a puritanical moral code. There were scandals, also, involving state lotteries in the nineteenth century. Moral or religious opposition is less intense today, although strong objections persist to the feared effects

---

1/ See U.S. President's Commission on Law Enforcement and the Administration of Justice, *The Challenge of Crime in a Free Society; A Report* (1967), p. 189.
2/ See *Newsweek*, April 10, 1972, p. 48.

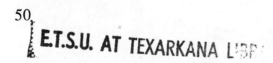

of addiction to games of chance—ruin for compulsive gamblers and impoverishment of those least able to afford the risks. But larger segments of the population—in all probability a majority—now reject the traditional code, and consider the total prohibition to be an irrational infringement upon personal freedom.

All states except Nevada forbid organized forms of gambling, although several have repealed references to private, casual, or charitable situations. The variance among state codes is confusing. The difficulty is magnified by the mobility of the population, and by the fact that so many laws are disregarded. Few Americans know the precise terms of the law supposedly governing their actions.

The inclination of tens of millions of citizens to bet on horse races, "the numbers," or team sports has led to formation of large criminal syndicates. Millions of small bets build a big business. Organized gambling is concentrated mainly in slums and ghettos, in hidden horse rooms, or with "bookies," out of sight of those most opposed to gambling on moral grounds. Complicity, or at least a benign blindness, on the part of police and other officials is essential to successful conduct of these illicit activities. Tacit toleration or "protective" arrangements with police can corrupt an entire force. Conspiracy is screened behind token arrests, and arrests to extort pay-offs, with occasional mild penalties for minor figures.

The extent of collusion varies from city to city and from one part of the country to another. Its range and depth within the nation's largest police force emerges, however, from the findings of two concurrent investigating commissions in New York City. Testimony indicates that new recruits hesitate to report gambling "payoffs" made to colleagues and superiors, and that the easy path is toward participation. Police involvement in gambling corruption is an entering wedge that leads quite readily to collusion in other profitable fields, such as the narcotics traffic. A recent feature in *The New York Times* offered historical perspective:[1]

> The history of the New York Police Department can be read as one long story of corruption. Every 20 years or so, there is a new scandal, followed by a brief flurry of reform, followed by the long gradual slide back into what seems to be the Department's normal state of discreet but all-pervasive corruption. . . .

1/ *The New York Times*, August 29, 1971, Section 4, page 6.

Virtually all policemen, for example, are convinced that a major corrupting influence would be removed if the laws against gambling could be eliminated.

Until this country comes to grips with the gambling issue, organized crime will prosper. Several courses of action are open. One is a serious, nationwide effort at suppression. Another is simple repeal of all statutes making gambling a crime. A third is governmental regulation and licensing. The fourth is provision of gambling facilities under direct governmental auspices, exemplified to some extent in several state lotteries and the off-track betting experiment in New York City.

STERN SUPPRESSION has many advocates, including some dedicated law enforcement officials. The strongest argument in its support rests on the exploitive nature of gambling, whether immoral or not. Some Western cities appear to have had success in such an effort. However, outright suppression seems well-nigh impossible in most larger cities, particularly in view of widespread police and other official involvement. Furthermore, determined attempts at rigid enforcement encounter strenuous opposition from large segments of the population.

Before suppression could be successful, a clear line would have to be drawn between forms of gambling considered permissible and those defined as criminal. Criminal codes in many states make *all* wagers on uncertain events and games of chance or skill illegal. Such strictures include private card games, casual bets on the golf course, pools or bets on athletic events and elections, and similar activities. An official crackdown on these practices is inconceivable; participants often do not know that they are engaged in criminal conduct. Raffles and bingo games conducted by charitable or church organizations are legal in some states; elsewhere, enforcement ranges from nonexistent or sporadic to stringent, leading in either case to criticism of law enforcement officials.

More than half of the states, including nine of the ten largest, sanction parimutuel betting on horse races at the tracks with little evidence of public opposition. In 1970, the parimutuel "handle" from legal bets at horse and greyhound tracks was $6.7 billion, of which the states retained $539 million in revenue. Newspapers everywhere publish the odds of payoffs. Annual racetrack attendance greatly exceeds that of all professional and collegiate football, baseball, and boxing contests combined. Yet off-track betting is a criminal offense except in Nevada and New York.

52

Certain gambling activities were made federal crimes in 1970, as part of an attack upon organized crime.[1] Arrests and prosecutions have begun. This federal initiative recognizes the need for skilled investigators in challenging gangsters engaged in conspiratorial crimes. Conceivably, it might be possible at least to inhibit the numbers rackets in central cities, bookmaking on races, football and baseball pools, and other forms of organized gambling. But the difficulties would be great, costs exorbitant, and the political implications serious. The national experiment with prohibition of alcoholic beverages is instructive. Repeal occurred after it became clear that moral codes opposed by major elements in the population are not enforceable by law. By that time, enforcement agencies had been deeply corrupted, while smuggling and bootlegging had laid the foundations for organized crime as a powerful force in America.

SIMPLE LEGALIZATION of gambling, by repeal of all references to it in the criminal codes, is an alternative without advocates. This action would not create a new source of public revenue, which is an objective of many willing to disturb the *status quo*. It might eliminate much of the official corruption now plaguing the nation, but it would leave in place exploitive organizations now exercising monopolistic privileges. Introduction of aggressive competition might also expand clienteles and increase patronage, but this is not desired by reform elements.

REGULATION THROUGH LICENSING has long been in effect in Nevada, where it produces 40 per cent of state revenues, and in the United Kingdom, although a shift toward governmental operation is under consideration there. The Commonwealth of Puerto Rico has permitted off-track betting and casino operations for decades, under strict licensing. The Nevada experience has not encouraged imitation, however. It is clouded by frequent scandals; public officials are accused of issuing licenses to persons and organizations of low repute, and failing to prevent "skimming" or fraudulent tax reports. Having legalized organized gambling (while prohibiting private gambling), Nevada has attracted a large corps of professional gamblers, many with unsavory reputations. It is a central location for major illicit gambling operations

---

[1] The Organized Crime Control Act of 1970, Title VIII, defines illegal gambling business as one which violates a state law, involves five or more persons, and operates for more than 30 days, or has a gross income of more than $2,000 in a single day. It also makes it a federal crime for a law enforcement officer to plot with a person engaged in illegal gambling to obstruct enforcement of anti-gambling laws.

conducted elsewhere. Licensed gambling has given Nevada a bad name, and *vice versa*.

Parimutuel betting at racetracks, another example of public control through licensing, has been less subject to such difficulties. However, large-scale off-track gambling on the same races, which is illegal, places pressures on legislatures and on other officials. Track locations, hidden ownerships, and allocations of racing days are handled in ways leaving the public suspicious of officials whose decisions have heavy financial impacts.

GOVERNMENTAL OPERATION of gambling facilities is quite new in this country, but rapid extension seems likely. It has taken two forms: state lotteries intended, sometimes unsuccessfully, to replace the "numbers" rackets; and off-track betting as a substitute for illicit bookmaking.

New Hampshire, New York, New Jersey, and Pennsylvania operate lotteries. Massachusetts and Connecticut have adopted enabling legislation, and several other states are considering such action. New Hampshire and New York have had limited success, due to serious weaknesses: (1) drawings are infrequent, in contrast to daily or weekly numbers drawings, and waiting time for announcement of awards is too long; (2) minimum ticket prices are too high, compared with the nickle-dime-quarter numbers patterns; (3) ticket outlets are not readily available in areas convenient to those who play the numbers; (4) payouts are a much smaller percentage of receipts than the 60 per cent customary for the illicit numbers rackets; and (5) the lotteries provide no credit arrangements or attractive personal relationships like those between numbers runners and players. Moreover, prizes are subject to federal and state income taxes.

Most of these weaknesses have been overcome by New Jersey, which has had a strong initial response to its lottery plan launched in 1971. Odds are reasonable and drawings are frequent. Tickets may be purchased in strips and in small denominations, at accessible locations. Within six months, coincident with a strong federal anti-rackets effort, the newspapers reported a 60 per cent reduction in patronage of New Jersey's numbers rackets and an anticipated annual state revenue of $160,000,000.

The newest, and perhaps most important, governmental initiative in this field is the establishment of state-operated off-track parimutuel betting by New York. Initial popular reaction appears to be favorable, arousing active interest in other states. Whether or not complete substitution for illicit horse rooms is possible, this pioneering effort will be closely watched—particularly in view of pressing needs for new sources of state and local revenue.

Illicit gambling, organized crime, and official collusion pose interconnected problems of grave proportions. Strong measures will be required to bring the situation under effective control. Moral attitudes, deeply held, make it difficult to find solutions commanding consensus. Answers simply have to be found, however, since public confidence in the integrity of government is at stake.

All statutes and ordinances that make unorganized (and charitable-religious) gambling criminal should be repealed; efforts to prohibit conduct socially acceptable to tens of millions of citizens are unjustifiable as well as unenforceable.

We recommend extensive experimentation with governmental ownership and operation of gambling arrangements that substitute effectively for the numbers rackets, horse rooms, and betting pools that now form the main source of income for organized crime. Experiments monitored and found successful should be widely copied by other states.*

This implies opening of public facilities easily accessible by location and by telephone for parimutuel betting on races and athletic events, and for frequent "numbers" drawings with tickets available in small denominations. Prizes should be commensurate with receipts, less modest overhead charges, and always above prevailing illicit odds levels. Funds derived by the states from these sources could be put to appropriate use in financing improvement of their judicial and correctional systems.

Federal and state income tax laws should be amended to exempt winnings from these governmental lotteries and parimutuels, for three reasons: illicit operations will otherwise enjoy an undeserved advantage; amounts wagered have already been subjected to tax deductions, and total winnings are always less than total losses because of subtraction of taxes and overhead from the parimutuel pools; losses should be deductible if winnings are taxed, but that would create opportunity for false claims of losses not actually incurred. Thus, if taxation of winnings is attempted, total tax yields would probably be lower, not higher.

It is not proposed, however, to make gains from illicit organized gambling legally tax-exempt.

---

*See Memorandum by MR. CHARLES KELLER, JR., page 77.

We reject extension of the concept of licensing for organized gambling, beyond its present use in parimutuel betting at race tracks, because of the Nevada experience involving the dubious character qualifications of licensees and the pressures on the authorities who manage the licensing.

Efforts by federal, state, and local governments to stamp out syndicated gambling operations should be accelerated, although only limited success can be anticipated pending provision of governmental gambling facilities.

Special emphasis should be placed upon rooting out official corruption, through expanded internal inspectional forces and through stronger legislation, as in California, against failure by police officers to report criminal gambling operations of which they have knowledge.

We also recommend, in the public schools and elsewhere, an educational campaign designed to portray the financial hazards and disadvantages of participation in gambling activities, stressing the odds and probabilities against the player.

Formation or continuation of gambling habits should be discouraged by means other than criminal penalties. Public gambling facilities are favored only because they appear to be the best alternative to the grip of the crime syndicates and the official corruption associated with them.

7.

GAINING THE CONSENT
OF THE GOVERNED

THE DECLARATION OF INDEPENDENCE advanced the proposition that governments derive their just powers from the consent of the governed. But great numbers of Americans do not now consent, in the least, to many of their laws nor to the manner of their enforcement. Conduct that citizens do not believe injurious to the community is defined as criminal and repressed, while assaults on persons and property go unpunished.* Distrusting the agencies of law enforcement, many citizens have lost all sense of personal responsibility for support and assistance to the authorities.

A law-abiding society, "with liberty and justice for all," can exist only when the overwhelming majority accepts and respects the laws—and aids their enforcement. To reach this goal, three kinds of change are needed: (1) Criminal codes must be made to conform to the prevailing public consensus on what conduct should be forbidden by law, and on the appropriate penalties. (2) Discriminatory enforcement must cease, as a first step in reducing racial and class animosities between officers of the law and major population groups. (3) Acting as community leaders, businessmen must recognize their own responsibility for law observance and offer support in enforcing the whole

*See Memorandum by MR. THEODORE O. YNTEMA, page 77.

57

range of criminal laws—including those concerned with offenses by business firms and by their officers and employees. White collar crimes of many descriptions pose a growing danger to society, a danger that deeply disturbs many members of the younger generation as well as most of their responsible elders.

Modernizing the Laws

The laws must be revised more frequently, for two reasons. The conditions of life are changing rapidly, and so are public attitudes concerning morality and criminal conduct. This has to be recognized if the processes of alienation are to be arrested. More revisions have been made in the criminal codes over the past decade than in any similar period, but changes have not kept pace with events. Worse, administration of the codes is often erratic, discriminatory, and ineffective. Very serious offenses may be dealt with lightly, while inconsequential actions may be handled severely. Relative penalties provide bizarre contrasts.

One area of serious weakness is the treatment of drunken driving. Half of the 50,000 and more highway deaths each year involve at least one driver under the influence of alcohol. (Casualties resulting from driving under the influence of dangerous drugs—both legal and illegal—are unknown.) Yet, drunken driving is treated with amazing leniency. Civil damages may be levied, but there has been great reluctance to impose penalties comparable with those for other homicides and assaults, or to apply the effective English practice of testing drivers at random for symptoms of intoxication. Prison sentences are rarely invoked, and suspension of licenses has not proved adequate. Such drivers must be kept off the highways; they should receive treatment as soon as facilities become available. Meanwhile, impoundment of the drunken driver's vehicle for a year might have a deterrent effect.

Criminal codes should be revised to impose appropriate penalties for driving under the influence of alcohol or dangerous drugs; enforcement should be meticulous and vigorous, using the best available detection devices.

Laws against concealed weapons and statutes requiring gun registration are also ineffective. Handguns exist for only one purpose: use against people. They account for over half of all murders. Nearly

58

all police killed in the line of duty die by handguns. Access to them is easy, in spite of sporadic and timid gestures toward control. Production, importation of parts for assembly, and distribution of these guns (and the ammunition for them) continues, with slight limitations, although deaths rise yearly. Wherever handguns are forbidden by well-enforced laws, abroad and in some American cities, murder rates are far lower. Flat prohibition of private possession of these weapons is clearly justified; those used by police and security forces or by others authorized to have them should be publicly owned.

Indemnification should be allowed—at federal expense—for owners who turn in their handguns to the authorities for destruction or governmental use, within a reasonable period of time. A provision would be made for retention of antiques, of course. These limitations should not be confused with attempts to license and control rifles or shotguns, strongly resisted by sportsmen and many other citizens.

Private importation, distribution, and possession of handguns and parts or ammunition for them should become major criminal offenses under both federal and state laws. The sole owners of such weapons should be the national and state governments, which could then issue them on a temporary and returnable basis to members of the security forces and other authorized persons under carefully drawn regulations. Manufacture should be halted until existing inventories are exhausted, after which further domestic production and export-import trade would be placed under strict licensing controls.

In contrast to weak treatment of actions that endanger life and safety stands the severity of laws dealing with behavior not considered really criminal by most citizens. For example, 113,400 arrests were made for vagrancy in 1970, and 1,825,500 for public intoxication (not involving drunken driving or a charge of disorderly conduct). These are "victimless" crimes. Chronic alcoholism calls for medical and psychiatric attention, not a criminal penalty. These arrests, subsequent prosecutions, court actions, and correctional controls divert valuable energy from protection of the public against more serious dangers.

Addiction to hard drugs (such as heroin, cocaine and amphetamines) is so destructive to the individual that it threatens society at large; it has spread rapidly among civilians and in the armed services. The need for money to support an expensive habit adds to rising rates of theft and robbery. The huge sums involved have led to corruption of federal agents and the police. Proper treatment for addicts and effective means for suppressing this traffic are both essential. The United Kingdom has had comparatively few addicts—perhaps because it provides heroin for those in maintenance and withdrawal programs, thus reducing incentives of purveyors to foster addiction. Experimental use of methadone (also addictive) as a heroin substitute has had some success in this country; other efforts at suppression have had unsatisfactory results.

The state codes, however, do not make suitable distinctions between extremely dangerous substances and others not addictive and of doubtful danger—such as marijuana. There is no present evidence that use of marijuana, which is nonaddictive, is as damaging physically or mentally as alcohol, nicotine, or tranquilizers—all addictive but legally and readily available. This was verified by two major 1972 reports, one submitted to Congress by the National Institute of Mental Health and the other submitted to the President and Congress by the Commission on Marijuana and Drug Abuse. Yet, possession of marijuana is a felony in most states; first offenders have been sentenced to prison terms of 20 years or more, and marijuana accounts for many more arrests than the hard drugs. A high proportion of the nation's youth make experimental or habitual use of marijuana, becoming criminals under the laws and so placing themselves in flagrant opposition to public authority. This undermines the foundations of society.

Criminal codes must be revised to conform with the present views of the American people concerning "criminal" conduct, and to rationalize penalties. Each state that does not have one should establish a commission on revision of its criminal code, to be appointed by the governor and including legislators and judges as well as public members. To secure prompt action, these commissions—and those committees of state legislatures that apply—should be funded in the entirety by the national government.

Bringing Police and Citizenry Together

Attention was called in chapter 4 to negative attitudes toward the police and other officers of the law, strongly held by groups in neighborhoods most subject to victimization and in greatest need of police protection. Unprovoked, random, and deadly assaults on policemen are an increasingly familiar phenomenon. Racial and ethnic minorities in the inner cities generally complain of two things: relative neglect in police protection and discriminatory treatment. High crime rates among these constituencies reinforce negative police attitudes, which are then in turn reciprocated.

A newer and perhaps an even more dangerous development is the intense hostility between large numbers of young middle or upper class Americans and the police. Alienation of the nation's youth is a serious matter. Revision of the criminal codes would help, but the main complaint is against inequity and injustice in law enforcement. Equality before the law is a fundamental precept. Cynical disregard of this principle will ultimately destroy American society, and there are signs that this deterioration may have begun.

We have stressed the need for professionalization of police management to minimize bias and prevent lawless conduct. There are frequent allegations of excessive force in making arrests, illegal interrogation and detention procedures, and systematic concealment of police misconduct and corruption. Instances of such behavior, found in many communities, have tarnished the police image. It may do more harm than good to urge ghetto youths to respect the law when those sworn to uphold it are seen to violate it frequently, openly, and with impunity.

We reemphasize the need to intensify efforts to professionalize the police and other agencies of law enforcement, and thus improve citizen-official relationships.

The Challenge to Business Leadership

A striking address on "Crime—a Businessman's Challenge" before a 1969 conference of American business leaders concluded with these words:

Today our country is grievously afflicted by a problem which daily grows larger. This affects our businesses. But far more important, it affects the quality of life in America. It engenders fear, distrust, lack of faith in government. It is not a good climate for business; it is not a good climate for living.

If we are to change this situation, all of us will have to get involved. You, as business leaders, are in the vanguard of every important social effort in the country; you will have to take leadership roles in this field, too.[1]

---

[1] Address by Richard L. Gelb, President of Bristol-Myers Company, a Trustee of CED, and a member of CED's Committee for Improvement of Management in Government.

The problem worsens. The U.S. Department of Commerce estimates the total cost of crimes against business in 1971 at $16 billion (not including the business share of governmental expenditures), broken down as follows:[2]

Manufacturers	$1,800,000,000
Wholesalers	1,340,000,000
Retail Outlets	
Inventory Loss	4,010,000,000
Robbery, Burglary, Vandalism	775,000,000
Service Enterprises	2,000,000,000
Investment Banks	1,000,000,000
Credit Card Frauds	140,000,000
Cargo Thefts	1,500,000,000
Arson	206,000,000
Preventive Security Costs	3,300,000,000

Every citizen, particularly those in leadership positions, must lend full support to necessary reforms if the explosive growth in crimes of all kinds is to be halted and reversed. This is doubly true of businessmen, who have unusual community influence and whose enterprises are the primary targets of lawlessness—through internal thefts, shoplifting, vandalism, and the depredations of organized crime.

Regrettably, the business community has hesitated to use the machinery of public law enforcement in its own defense. Firms often rely upon security bonds and theft insurance to protect against loss, not concerning themselves with ultimate justice. Prosecution of employees who embezzle or pilfer has seemed more trouble than it is worth. Time taken by employees to testify in court against offenders is grudgingly allowed. And fear of retaliation inhibits business collaboration in suppression of the syndicates. It must be conceded that some businessmen have a general philosophy that the fewer their contacts with government, for whatever purpose, the better. But silence is a form of complicity. Civic responsibility coincides with the necessities of self-defense.

Individually, businessmen can clean their own houses. Organized gambling need not be tolerated on business premises; labor leaders (except those tied to the rackets) will usually cooperate. Loan-sharking

---

[2] U.S. Department of Commerce, *The Economic Impact of Crimes Against Business* (February, 1972).

can be countered when employees have access to proper credit facilities. Internal thefts can be reported promptly, and the prosecutor in such cases should have full support. Whenever the odor of organized criminal activity is noted either inside or outside a business, confidential channels for a full report to completely dependable agencies of law enforcement can and should be found and used.

Individually and collectively, business leaders can speak out for changes needed to reverse the present course of events. They can support those in government at every level and in all three branches—legislative, executive, and judicial—who are actively seeking these changes. The weight of their influence can be brought to bear both publicly and behind the scenes to make sure that the law enforcement agencies are properly managed, competently and incorruptibly staffed, and adequately financed.

Criminal justice planning bodies have been or are being established at state and local levels; businessmen should seek membership on them. They can also cooperate in probation and parole projects that offer hope for rehabilitation of offenders, including those recovering from alcohol or drug addiction. In these matters and in the conduct of their enterprises, businessmen can show a greater awareness and a deeper concern for the public interest.

Every businessman should take an active role in improving the administration of criminal justice. A prompt and complete report of every known criminal offense should be made whether committed by employees, company officers, customers, or elements of organized crime. Aid should be given in prosecution of offenders.

Governmental authority at every level should provide secure confidential channels for reports on suspected syndicate activities, assuring active investigation. Business organizations should offer plans for action and mutual assistance in these matters.

* * * *

Means must be found to bring the people and their official agents into closer harmony. Justice and the consent of the governed cannot exist apart from each other. The obligations are mutual. Agencies of law enforcement must establish higher professional standards of trust and dependability, and the citizenry with its leadership must support necessary statutory and institutional reforms. Business leaders should be found in the front rank of those dedicated to equal justice and faithful execution of the laws.

8.

CLEARING THE HURDLE
OF FEDERALISM

IECEMEAL REFORM of the patchwork structure of criminal justice will fail; a more fundamental approach must be taken. The highly complex multilevel federal system, evolved from simpler beginnings, has its merits—but an ability to solve the American crime problem is not among them. The present intricate division of responsibilities, functions, and financial support among national, state, and local levels is the chief barrier to acceptable patterns of criminal justice. Drastic changes in these arrangements are needed, but our proposals, while overcoming existing obstacles, would retain the basic element in the federal concept—a close cooperation between the nation and the states.

The twin goals of order and justice can be achieved only through a redistribution of primary functions, together with internal reorganizations at state and national levels. Local governments, overburdened with a multitude of problems beyond their resources and capabilities, should be relieved of all obligations for administration of criminal justice, except for the maintenance of police forces and, perhaps, pre-trial detention. The states should exercise their legal powers more actively, and undertake direct management of courts, prosecutions, and all correctional activities—along with a larger share of the police function. They should adjust their organizational patterns to facilitate these changes.

The national government must give strong leadership and large financial aid to relieve a crisis that is clearly nationwide. We believe the best, and perhaps the only, means of achieving these objectives is the establishment of a Federal Authority To Ensure Justice, endowed with powers and resources needed for its crucial role. We see this as the capstone in the structure of American justice, renewed and revitalized.

Strengthening State Capabilities

The states have enacted the basic criminal codes but rely for enforcement upon the tangle of overlapping local jurisdictions they have spawned. The chief concern of state police is with traffic control; they seldom provide more than minimal assistance to local forces. Governors and attorneys general exercise only slight influence over local prosecutions for violations of state laws. Few states have moved toward unified court systems or assumed total responsibility for corrections. All this must change.

The nation's 3,000 counties should no longer play a major role in administering criminal justice. Most of them are too small in population and resources to cope effectively with dangerous new conditions. Even the largest of them elect their sheriffs, prosecutors, and coroners by partisan ballot; deputies and assistants lack tenure and are rarely chosen on the basis of merit. Agencies organized along such archaic lines can hardly be expected to meet the tests of trying times. With the problems of large cities approaching crisis proportions, their revenues shrink as jobs and residents move to the suburbs. Some have adequate police forces; most do not. Smaller cities, villages, towns, and townships suffer from the same inabilities as most counties—while the tides of suburban-rural criminal activity are rising. Public support for law enforcement at this level is more often verbal than financial. Moreover, the federal and state aid already given has often been misused.

Drastic changes are in order. We have proposed that the states relieve local governments of *all responsibility* for maintenance of courts, the prosecution function, and post-conviction imprisonment. Further, we have urged expansion of state police forces, organized either centrally or on a regional basis. Admittedly, as noted in CED's statement on *Modernizing State Government,* the states are poorly organized to manage even their present functions. To overcome this weakness while assuming a larger responsibility for criminal justice, each state should gather together and coordinate its separate units and agencies working in this field to form a coordinated system within a single Department of Justice.

This is the solution recommended in 1968 by the Joint Legislative Committee to Study Crime and the System of Criminal Justice in New Jersey. That Committee gave the following explanation of its concern:

> ... this Committee finds the system of administering criminal justice to be complex, fragmented both in functions and jurisdiction, undernourished, without focus or command, largely invisible as to what is really happening, nowhere near as effective as we believe it should be—and neglected.
>
> It is neglected in the largest and most important matters, such as leadership, drive and understanding.
>
> It is neglected in smaller but important matters as well, such as needed individual statutes or programs addressed to special problems where immediate action can be mounted. . . .
>
> *We recommend:* A New Jersey Department of Criminal Justice as the vital means of strengthening the entire system.

As proposed by this Joint Legislative Committee, the new Department of Criminal Justice would be responsible to the Governor, and would contain Divisions of Law Enforcement, Youth, Prosecution, Narcotic Addiction, and Rehabilitation, along with two staff Divisions—for Administration and Policy Planning. Consolidation of closely related functions would enlarge the opportunities for enlightened management. The judiciary would remain independent, of course; the courts are already largely unified in New Jersey.

We recommend that each of the 50 states establish a Department of Justice, drawing together all germane functions except those of a separate, independent, and unified judicial branch, with which the new Department could maintain close liaison.

Furthermore, we recommend that local units of government be relieved by the states of responsibilities for criminal justice, other than the maintenance of urban police forces.

A Federal Authority To Ensure Justice

Realistic citizens may accept the validity of the foregoing recommendations but still doubt that the states will adopt them in time. Therefore, we urge massive federal funding to aid the states (and local units)—but only on condition that acceptable standards of organization and performance are met. The national government has no constitutional responsibility or direct authority for general law enforcement. But when customary patterns of federalism break down in the face of critical and widespread problems, the people of this country have on many occasions turned to the national government. That breakdown is now evident. The national government has begun to respond, but only in tentative fashion and with slight actual effect. This response should be felt at two distinct levels: directly, through its own agencies; and through financial aid to states and local units.

The direct federal police effort is limited to enforcement of federal laws, covering a minor share of all criminal infractions. It is divided among several specialized units in four major departments not noted for close cooperation. Criticism has grown in recent years, both as to priorities and effectiveness. The Federal Bureau of Investigation is the largest of these forces, with the broadest jurisdiction. Internal subversive activities have been its main concern; acceptance of responsibility for suppression of organized crime and protection of civil rights was slow and reluctant.

Bureaus and divisions nominally under the Attorney General have a long tradition of jealous autonomy; interdepartmental cooperation is even harder to obtain. The inroads of organized crime have finally led to serious efforts to gain coordination, however, through a strike-force approach developed in 1967. These special task forces, now operative in a score of major cities, bring together the manpower and resources of several agencies. Typically, they include agents from the Bureau of Narcotics and Dangerous Drugs and the Immigration and Naturalization Service of the Department of Justice; the Internal Revenue Service, the Bureau of Customs, and the Secret Service of the Treasury Department; the Office of Labor-Management of the Department of Labor; and the Inspection Service of the U.S. Postal Service.

While the FBI has an annual budget of some $20 million to fight organized crime it has seldom assigned its agents to those strike-forces;

instead, it is said to cooperate with them—though at arms-length. The strike-forces operate independently of the United States Attorneys in most cases also, and contacts with state or local authorities are minimal (partly because of a justifiable fear of information leaks). Progress is encouraging, although the strength of the syndicates is not visibly impaired.

The Omnibus Crime Control and Safe Streets Act of 1968 initiated a vast new federal role. It created the Law Enforcement Assistance Administration, within the Department of Justice, to dispense federal grants-in-aid for improvement of state and local law enforcement. This agency was not well designed and its programs have been poorly administered. One mistake was to place LEAA under a triumvirate that could act only unanimously, leaving differences unresolved and vacancies unfilled until corrective legislation was enacted. Another mistake, even more damaging, was to channel most local aid through the state governments, despite the lack of state agencies qualified to manage the distribution. Most states allocated much of the money to jurisdictions with relatively few problems and for indefensible uses, while central cities with greatest need received proportionately less. Most of the money appropriated was never spent.

In the three years through June 30, 1971, LEAA was given total budget authority of $856 million. But actual outlays were only $327 million. This left $529 million—or 62 per cent—unspent. During the same three years, the states did "allocate" $521 million of LEAA money to "sub-grantees" (local governments). But of this only $139 million, or 27 per cent, was actually disbursed to them—leaving almost three-fourths of the allocations unused. Congressional hearings, moreover, have revealed numerous instances of funds distributed to state and local law enforcement units being put to inconsequential or frivolous uses.[1]

Besides its lack of any real sense of urgency, LEAA has been remiss in failure to define objectives and goals, to prescribe priorities, to enforce standards, and to audit performance. Its new National Advisory Commission on Criminal Justice Standards and Goals, created in 1971 "to fashion meaningful yardsticks for measuring progress," has constructive possibilities but no real power. While the states have set up law enforcement planning agencies, significant reforms are

---

[1] See U.S., Congress, House, Committee on Government Operations: *The Block Grant Programs of the Law Enforcement Assistance Program,* hearings before the Subcommittee on Legal and Monetary Affairs (1971).

68

conspicuously few. Mere channeling of money does not produce a coherent program for action nor the organizational means to effect it.

Benefits from this federal initiative have been far below expec-
tations. Crime rates have not fallen; they have risen, alarmingly, con-
tinuously in urban, suburban, and rural areas.[2] To understate the point,
measures taken to date have not furnished a solution. But the solution
must be found; the crisis cannot be shunted aside.

The national government must devise a national strategy to deal
with this nationwide problem. In the main, however, the actions taken
by the police, prosecutors, courts, and correctional agencies have to
occur at state or local levels. Hesitation and delay characterize the state
response to date, and there is little prospect of early improvement
unless heavy new pressures are brought to bear. Use of federal funds
for this purpose is imperative, with disbursement conditional upon
fundamental and thorough-going reform of the present "non-system"
of criminal justice at state and local levels of government.

No existing federal agency is suited to the management of this
monumental task. None has a range of interests comprehensive enough
to cover all the broad, interrelated elements. The Department of Justice
is in no position to assume this responsibility. It lacks essential jurisdiction in many fields; it has not adequately coordinated the autonomous bureaus nominally subordinate to it; and the record of LEAA
cited above does not inspire confidence in the Department's capacity
to give effective leadership to state-local law enforcement. With notable
exceptions, over the years top posts in the Department have been
heavily politicized, which is unfortunate in view of its intended role.
Its reputation weakens its influence with key Congressional committees
and with many state officials. More important, it undermines public
confidence in the system of justice. While there are other federal
departments which also have law enforcement functions, we believe
that none is fitted for this comprehensive assignment.

It is clear that a major new federal agency of unquestioned
stature must be established to achieve the necessary breakthrough in
this field. This recommendation accords with past experience; old-line
agencies with their built-in bureaucratic rigidities are seldom entrusted

---

2/ In 1968, murders, forcible rapes, robberies, and aggravated assaults known to the
police were estimated by the FBI at 589,000. The preliminary figure for 1971 approxi-
mates 800,000—an increase of 36 per cent in three years. Known burglaries, larcenies
over $50, and auto thefts rose from 3,878,000 in 1968 to about 5,125,000 in 1971,
up 32 per cent. See Appendix A for additional data.

with new and vital initiatives. The Federal Reserve was not placed under the Department of the Treasury, nor was the TVA made part of the Department of the Interior. Temporary units with vast powers were created to deal with national emergencies growing out of the depression of the 1930's, World War II, and the postwar reconversion. Having served their varied purposes, most of them were eventually folded into other segments of the executive establishment. This Committee is always reluctant to propose a new federal agency, but we can find no acceptable alternative that would meet the urgent necessity.

We recommend creation of a "Federal Authority To Ensure Justice," endowed with a sweeping range of statutory powers and generously funded by the national government, under a Board appointed by the President subject to Senate confirmation, with its chairman acting as chief executive officer.

Within broad statutory guidelines drawn by Congress, this Authority should be given powers to:

■ set and enforce the standards — substantive, administrative, and organizational—governing large federal grants-in-aid in support of all criminal justice functions;*

■ establish, organize, and direct administrative mechanisms to develop strategic plans and policies, evaluate performance of ongoing programs, and provide advisory and liaison services to state and local units;

■ formulate new legislative proposals, whenever necessary, and review pending legislation at the request of Congressional committees;

■ advance and finance educational programs on a broad front— including aids to academic institutions with appropriate programs in criminal justice and, if necessary, foundation of a federal staff college for the advancement of criminal justice— to assure suitable training for all law enforcement officers with discretionary functions, as a requirement for holding such positions;

■ commission or manage research into every aspect of this field deemed worthy of serious investigation;

■ make an annual Report to the President and Congress—comparable to that of the Council of Economic Advisers—describing

---

*See Memorandum by MR. HERMAN L. WEISS, page 75.

the national condition with regard to crime and justice and outlining policy directions; and

■ assure the collection and analysis of dependable, comprehensive, detailed data covering every aspect of criminal justice—either under its own or other suitable auspices.

It would be appropriate for the Authority to review the roles of the many separate organizational units of the national government concerned with the administration of criminal justice, examine their effectiveness, and propose beneficial changes. This is important because it is clear that the national government will have to take a more active part in many fields of law enforcement, such as suppression of the national and international traffic in hard drugs and handguns, and the activities of organized crime.

The chairman of the Authority should have charge of its extensive administrative operations. Board confirmation of his major appointments would be desirable. The LEAA as it exists should be transferred to the Authority's jurisdiction, serving as a nucleus for an expanded unit to manage large conditional grants. So should the Treasury Department's contemplated Consolidated Law Enforcement Training Center, for which Congress has appropriated $26 million of an eventual $52 million (although obligations have not been incurred pending further planning). Other federal agencies would remain in place pending intensive review of their operations. The chairman's position as a Presidential appointee would place him at the level where strong Presidential support could assist in dealing with other elements in the Executive Branch as well as the public.

The success of the Authority will greatly depend, of course, upon the quality and strength of the members of its board. The gravity of its responsibilities would surely lead the President to nominate outstanding citizens. Its role is so vital, however, that we believe it desirable to establish, by statute, an Advisory Commission of a dozen or more members which would meet with the Authority's board at monthly or quarterly intervals, to review progress and advise on major issues. Such a Commission, also appointed by the President, might well include retired justices of the U.S. Supreme Court, judges of high state courts, Members of Congress, governors and other state or local officials, together with public members held in high national esteem. The Commission would not go beyond an advisory role, but it would add prestige and expertise to the Authority, thus helping to obtain both public and Congressional support.

Meanwhile, the 50 states should progressively assume their full constitutional responsibility for conditions within their borders. The Authority would make available to them the full federal funding we have proposed for review and revision of state criminal codes. Sweeping structural reform of all aspects of the administration of criminal justice at state and local levels is required.

The proposed Authority should be empowered to provide grants-in-aid to the states for a major share—perhaps half—of the cost of unified state court systems, fully consolidated state correctional systems, and state-managed prosecutions, subject in each case to meeting prescribed standards. Furthermore, the Authority should make direct grants in support of all police forces—state and local—that satisfy reasonable standards of modernization and excellence.

These recommendations are made in full recognition of the costs that will have to be borne by the U.S. Treasury. Total annual expenditures for all criminal justice functions are now about $10 billion. Half of that sum would become a federal charge—most of it additional to present payments through LEAA—assuming that the states meet eligibility standards. The purpose would justify this expenditure in any case, but there would be an important by-product. Local government budgets would be primary beneficiaries of these federal aids, thus reducing the burden of property taxation. Property taxes and revenue sharing command such current interest that our proposals deserve examination in that light.

The actual distribution of public expenditures for criminal justice in 1969, between the three levels of government, is shown and analyzed in Appendix C.[3] The effect of our proposals on this distribution—assuming no changes in the relative amounts spent on the several functions—is also shown in that Appendix. With a static level of total expenditures, at $10 billion, our proposed distribution would increase the U.S. Treasury burden by $4.1 billion; local governments would be relieved of $3.6 billion, and the states would benefit by about $500 million.

---

[3] Just after this document had gone to press, the U.S. Department of Justice released financial statistics for fiscal 1969-70 showing that total direct expenditures for the administration of criminal justice had risen 16.8% from the previous year, to $8.6 billion. The proportionate share of national, state, and local governments in these expenditures were little changed, however, and this was also the case as to shares spent for police, courts, prosecution, and corrections. The argument presented in the text, therefore, remains unchanged.

72

This is not wholly realistic, of course, since we have urged improvements that would cost money—notably in corrections. An over-all increase of 20 per cent would bring total expenditures to about $12 billion (disregarding inflationary factors). The effect of this change would be to bring the increase in U.S. costs to $5.1 billion. But the local governments would remain the primary beneficiaries, both in better services and in reduced costs, which would still be $3 billion below the present level. The states would be spending about what they do now, but to far greater effect.

If changes are made, as they should be, in the relative shares of the four functions—courts, prosecution, police, and corrections—these estimates would be modified accordingly. For example, some cities may decide to separate local neighborhood police patrols from the central city force, and place them under local control—as suggested in CED's 1970 statement *Reshaping Government in Metropolitan Areas.* Under any conceivable rearrangement, however, the local governments would be relieved of a major expenditure burden. This, in turn, would give substantial relief for the primary local tax source, achieving one of the basic objectives of revenue sharing. At the same time, a great advance in crime control and the administration of justice can be achieved.

* * * *

It would be hard to exaggerate the enormity of the national predicament, as outlined in these pages. During the decade of the 1960's, Index crimes of violence known to the police rose 156 per cent, offenses against property 180 per cent. If these and other crimes are permitted to double or treble again in the 1970's, American society as we have known it cannot endure.

We do not regard the situation as hopeless; we would not have taken the pains to issue this statement if we did. But we do believe that only the strongest measures—such as those advocated herein—can avert a worse disaster than the one we already see about us. Hence the urgent need for prompt and powerful action to reform and restructure every aspect of the administration of criminal justice at all levels of government is made completely clear.

This nation cannot form a more perfect Union, nor establish justice, nor insure domestic tranquility by means of discriminatory and capricious application of obsolete penal codes. Archaic methods, incompetent or unprofessional conduct, failure to devise and carry

73

through coherent plans, cannot be condoned. Nor can corruption or collusion between criminals and officers of the law be tolerated any longer.

Now, as at our nation's beginning, our governments derive their just powers only from the consent of the governed. This implies a reconciliation between all instruments of government and the people—the people of all classes, all ages, all races, all circumstances of life. The mechanisms of criminal justice must, therefore, be made worthy of the faith and trust of modern men and women facing the many hazards of these changing times.

MEMORANDA OF COMMENT, RESERVATION, OR DISSENT

Pages 15 and 70—By HERMAN L. WEISS, with which WILLIAM H. ABBOTT has asked to be associated:

State and local adoption of federal standards of police, judicial, and penal administration, as a condition of obtaining federal grants, may well be the only way to bring about major reforms within a reasonable time. Yet this proposal to establish a substantial degree of federal control over the structure, staffing and policies of state courts, local and state police, prison systems, and even substantive criminal codes, is bound to meet with serious reservations, particularly if the standards (some of which are sure to be highly controversial) are to be set by appointive federal officials. The proposal might meet with somewhat less resistance if the principal standards were incorporated by Congress in the enabling legislation and so reflected the views of an elective body. In any case, the policy statement proposal will draw opposition from all the sources of opposition to state and local reform, plus some others as well. The business community and the public generally ought not to be lulled by the prospect of federal action, but should also press for early state and local consideration of the long overdue reforms recommended in this statement.

Page 20—By ALEXANDER L. STOTT:

This recommendation seems inadequate in the light of the preceding discussion of the causes of court congestion. I would not disagree with a recommendation that more judges should be added where they are needed to speed up the judicial process. However, I feel that an equally strong recommendation should urge the improvement of court management, and it should urge federal and state legislators to provide adequate funds for such improvement programs.

Page 22—By ALEXANDER L. STOTT:

Ineffectiveness on the part of the chief judge is far more critical to the court than in any other position. Thus, if the chief judge is given administrative authority as outlined in the previous recommendation, some process could be considered providing for withdrawal of the assignment of a particular judge as the chief judge in his court if he is found to lack the capacity for leadership and management necessary for that function.

Page 22—By ALEXANDER L. STOTT:

This recommendation expresses a desirable goal, but it would need more than a simple directive to implement it. The federal system is only about one-tenth of the size of state and local judiciaries, and it is difficult to imagine that the Administrative Office of the U.S. Courts could handle the suggested data gathering function without great augmentation of the staff and even then with efficiency. State and local judicial systems lend themselves to computer operations and these systems should be exploited for their data gathering capacity before attempting to place this burden on the federal system.

Page 46—By DONALD S. PERKINS:

Any CED policy statement on *Reducing Crime and Assuring Justice* should comment on whether capital punishment is appropriate for even the most terrible of crimes. Elsewhere in this statement it is suggested that practices which are acceptable to vast numbers of our citizens should not be legislated against. Presumably the reverse is also true. I have not been convinced that the existence of the death penalty has had any real impact to reduce violent crimes. As a way of removing people from society it may be less expensive than incarceration, but it is probably not in keeping with the feelings of most of our citizens who might agree that capital punishment is unnecessarily barbaric. What I would like to have seen the report recommend is the abolition of the death penalty and its replacement by longer jail sentences than are now the case and that these sentences not be subject to parole for a significant number of years.

We would therefore be recommending an approach to a true life sentence for those whose actions require that they be separated from society.

Page 55—By CHARLES KELLER, JR.:

Although I approve the Statement, I have considerable reservation about Chapter 6 concerning organized gambling, perhaps because it is such a complex issue. It is proposed for example to legalize charitable-religious gambling, yet I have read of instances where such gambling had been taken over by professional gamblers, who have "skimmed" most of the proceeds leaving little or nothing for the charitable-religious institution, so that the institution was in fact merely a legal cover for an illicit operation. Nor can I justify exempting gambling winnings from income tax liability. This seems to provide an unnecessary additional incentive for gambling. Finally it seems to me that the 1970 federal legislation directed against organized gambling should be given an opportunity to operate before large additional new initiatives are undertaken.

I am most apprehensive about the long term results of widespread large government-operated gambling institutions with all the opportunities for fraud and corruption that are inherent in such operations.

Page 57—By THEODORE O. YNTEMA:

This policy statement goes part way in its treatment of "victimless crimes"; I believe it should go all the way. Approximately half of all arrests are for such victimless acts. In addition, a substantial portion of crimes against property and person are drug connected. Organized crime derives its main support from providing services, now illegal, that a large number of citizens want. If we abolished "victimless crimes" by legalizing such acts (subject where necessary to appropriate controls), our court calendars could be cleared, our resources for control of crime could be devoted to protection of person and property, and organized crime would have much less opportunity to flourish. We could then also do better in our efforts to help those suffering from drug, alcoholic or gambling addiction.

APPENDICES

◆

Appendix A: THE EXTENT OF CRIME

Statistics on crime in the United States are incomplete and deficient. The FBI first began to develop its "Uniform Crime Reports" in 1933, but even today many local police forces fail to supply factual information. State definitions of crimes differ, creating problems in assembly of "uniform" data. The FBI's Crime Index includes only seven major offenses; reports on other crimes usually cover only limited areas and only arrest data. Moreover, many crimes are never reported, and records on reports received vary from place to place and between classes of victims. Methods of handling doubtful cases can result in substantial differences in "rates," making statistical "crime waves," or the opposite, possible without any actual change in conditions.

Despite limitations, published data do have significance in national, regional, and urban *vs.* rural comparisons. Crime rates have risen dramatically over the past decade, far more rapidly than would be explained by population growth, either total or for the crime-prone 15-24 age group. This is shown in the following table, derived from the FBI's *Uniform Crime Reports.*

Moreover, opinion research inquiries using a representative sample of the population showed in 1965 that crimes actually committed exceeded those officially reported, by 50 per cent for robberies, by 100 per cent for aggravated assaults, and by nearly 300 per cent for forcible rapes. There were also twice as many larcenies and three times as many burglaries as shown in the FBI reports from which the above data were drawn.

79

Appendix A: OFFENSES KNOWN TO POLICE*

	1960	1970	Increase	Estimated Arrests 1970
Criminal homicide	9,000	15,812	+ 75.7%	15,230
Forcible rape	16,860	37,273	+121.1%	19,050
Robbery	107,390	348,380	+224.4%	98,210
Aggravated assault	152,000	329,937	+117.1%	155,060
4 Crimes of Violence	285,250	731,402	+156.5%	**287,550**
Burglary	897,400	2,169,322	+141.7%	358,100
Larceny over $50	506,200	1,746,107	+244.9%	748,200
Auto theft	325,700	921,366	+182.9%	153,300
3 Crimes against Property	1,729,300	4,836,795	+179.6%	**1,259,600**

Other Offenses Against Property

Vandalism	141,900
Fraud	104,600
Buying, receiving, possessing stolen property	74,000
Forgery and counterfeiting	55,500
Arson	11,900
Embezzlement	10,000

Other Offenses

Drunkenness	1,825,500
Disorderly conduct	710,000
Driving under influence of alcohol	555,700
Other assaults, not aggravated	348,900
Narcotic drug laws	415,600
Liquor laws	309,000
Vagrancy	113,400
Carrying or possessing weapons, etc.	120,400
Gambling	91,700
Offenses against family and children	78,500
Sex offenses (except forcible rape and prostitution)	59,700
Prostitution and commercialized vice	51,700
All other offenses (except traffic)	1,492,590

GRAND TOTAL, ALL ARRESTS (except traffic)	**8,117,740**

* Partially estimated.

Appendix B: CRIMINAL JUSTICE STRUCTURE IN THE UNITED STATES

	National Government	State Governments (50)	County Governments (3,050)	Municipal (18,000) and other Governments
I. POLICE FORCES	FBI (17,300 people) Bureau of Narcotics (2,000 people) Border Patrol (1,500) IRS-Tax Fraud, etc. (2,900) IRS-Alcohol, etc. (2,000) Treasury-Secret Service (2,500) Customs (1,400) Park Police (1,200) Sky Marshals (2,000) TOTALS. These and other units, full-time equivalent 1969: 35,500 persons	State police and highway patrols 1969 employment, full-time equivalent: 53,500 persons	Elective sheriffs and a few separate police depts.	About 35,000 separate police forces
			Total 1969 employment, full-time equivalent: 377,200 persons. Of these, 15-20% are county employees, 80-85% work for municipal, township, or other governmental levels.	
			In 1967, there were 58,400 full-time and 8,400 part-time county employees	In 1967, there were 154,400 full-time and 41,600 part-time municipal employees, plus 5,900 full-time and 16,500 part-time township employees, in addition to 3,500 full-time and 9,000 part-time special district employees

Appendix B: CRIMINAL JUSTICE STRUCTURE IN THE UNITED STATES (Continued)

	National Government	State Governments (50)	County Governments (3,050)	Municipal (18,000) and other Governments
II. PROSECUTION	93 District Attorneys' offices 1969 full-time equivalent employment: 5,800 plus 1,800 in indigent defense	50 Attorneys General 1969 full-time equivalent employment: 6,400	Some 3,000 Elective Prosecuting Attorneys (District Attorneys, State's Attorneys, etc.)	Usually depend, in serious offenses, on county prosecution
			1969 full-time employment equivalent: 21,800 plus 2,100 engaged in indigent defense	
III. COURTS	U.S. Supreme Court 10 Circuit Courts of Appeals 93 District Courts Special Tax, Customs, Claims Courts 1969 full-time equivalent employment: 5,800	50 State Supreme Courts Intermediate Courts of Appeals Circuit and other Courts of Original Jurisdiction 1969 full-time equivalent employment: 15,600	Uncounted numbers of lower courts, mainly with original jurisdiction, including county courts, magistrates' courts, justices of the peace, together with special courts on traffic, domestic relations, juvenile offenders, etc. 1969 full-time equivalent employment: 63,700	

Appendix B: CRIMINAL JUSTICE STRUCTURE IN THE UNITED STATES (Continued)

	National Government	State Governments (50)	County Governments (3,050)	Municipal (18,000) and other Governments
IV. CORRECTIONS	1969 full-time equivalent employment: 5,400	1969 full-time equivalent employment: 84,600	1969 full-time equivalent employment: 48,500	
			1967 employment: 32,400 full-time and 2,700 part-time	1967 municipal employment: 11,000 full-time and 200 part-time
	Prison population, Dec. 31, 1967: 19,500	Prison population, Dec. 31, 1967: 175,300	Prison population, March 15, 1970, held in some 4,000 local jails: 160,900, of whom 75,000 were awaiting trial	

Appendix C:

A PROPOSAL FOR A BETTER DISTRIBUTION
OF THE COSTS OF CRIMINAL JUSTICE

In addition to the considerations which made necessary the recommendations for a decreased role for local governments in the administration of criminal justice—the demands for unified, coherent, professional administration on a statewide level—is the simple fact that local governments, particularly those of the large cities, cannot afford the costs. Their finances rest primarily on badly administered and inequitable property taxes based on rapidly declining property values in those areas where the need for better services is the greatest.

Total public expenditures for the criminal justice function were distributed in fiscal 1969—the most recent year for which detailed figures are available—as shown in the first table, below. The effect of our proposals on the distribution—assuming no changes in the relative amounts spent on the several functions—is shown in the second table.

DIVISION OF COSTS, ADMINISTRATION OF CRIMINAL JUSTICE, by Level of Government. Actual, Fiscal 1969

Level of Government	Courts	Prosecution and Defense	Police	Corrections	TOTALS
National	1.4%	1.8%	6.7%	1.0%	10.9%
State	3.2	1.1	8.5	12.4	25.2
Local	9.0	3.2	45.2	6.5	63.9
TOTALS	13.6%	6.1%	60.4%	19.9%	100.0%

		Proposed, Future Years			
Level of Government	Courts	Prosecution and Defense	Police	Corrections	TOTALS
National	7.5%	3.95%	31.15%	8.8%	51.4%
State	6.1	2.15	4.25	7.8	20.3
Local	—	—	25.0[a]	3.3[a]	28.3
TOTALS	13.6%	6.1%	60.4%	19.9%	100.0%

[a] *It is assumed that about one-ninth of local police costs would be borne 100% locally, for failure to meet federal standards. It is also assumed that local jails would continue to house persons awaiting trial, at local expense, with state assumption of responsibility for those convicted.*

Assuming a static level of total expenditures at $10 billion, our proposed distribution of costs would increase the U.S. Treasury burden by $4.1 billion; local governments would be relieved of $3.6 billion, and the states of about $500 million.

But recommended improvements would cost additional money—notably in corrections. An over-all increase of 20 per cent would bring total expenditures to about $12 billion (disregarding inflationary factors). The effect of this change would be to bring the increase in U.S. costs to $5.1 billion, reducing the net local benefit to $3 billion and leaving the states at about their present levels of expenditures.

If changes are made in the relative expenditure shares of the four functions—courts, prosecution, police, and corrections—these estimates would have to be modified accordingly. However, under any conceivable rearrangement, the local governments would be relieved of a major expenditure burden now imposed by them mainly upon property owners.

ADDED FEDERAL COSTS AND STATE-LOCAL BENEFITS
At a $10 billion level

	Annual Rates in billions of dollars		
	Actual 1969 Distribution	CED's Proposed Distribution	Gain or (Loss)
National	$ 1.1	$ 5.2	(−$4.1)
State	2.5	2.0	+ 0.5
Local	6.4	2.8	+ 3.6
	$10.0	$10.0	0.0

At a $12 billion level

	Annual Rates in billions of dollars	
	CED's Proposed Distribution	Gain or (Loss) Compared with $10 billion Actual 1969
National	$ 6.2	(−$5.1)
State	2.4	+ 0.1
Local	3.4	+ 3.0
	$12.0	(−$2.0)

CED Board of Trustees

HONORARY TRUSTEES

PUBLICATION ORDER FORM

To order CED publications please indicate number in column entitled "# Copies Desired." Then mail this order form and check for total amount in envelope to Distribution Division, CED, 477 Madison Ave., New York 10022.

SEE OTHER SIDE→

ORDER NUMBER		# COPIES DESIRED

33P . . NONTARIFF DISTORTIONS OF TRADE $1.00 _____
Examines the complex problem of dealing with nontariff distortions of trade arising
from governmental measures that create special barriers to imports and incentives
to exports.

32P . . FISCAL AND MONETARY POLICIES FOR STEADY ECONOMIC GROWTH $1.00 _____
Reexamines the role of fiscal and monetary policies in achieving the basic economic
objectives of high employment, price stability, economic growth, and equilibrium
in the nation's international payments.

31P . . FINANCING A BETTER ELECTION SYSTEM $1.00 _____
Urges comprehensive modernization of election and campaign procedures at
national, state, and local levels. Proposes ways to reduce costs and spread them
more widely through tax credits.

30P . . INNOVATION IN EDUCATION $1.00 _____
Examines the problems of the American schools, reviews educational goals and
opportunities (including technological resources), and explores relative costs and
benefits. Sets forth comprehensive recommendations for change.

28P . . MODERNIZING STATE GOVERNMENT $1.00 _____
Recommends sweeping renovation of state governments and their constitutions. Proposes granting legislatures broad powers to deal with problems of a rapidly-changing
era; strengthening executive capability through modern management methods; improving the administration of justice; and furthering intergovernmental relations.

27P . . TRADE POLICY TOWARD LOW-INCOME COUNTRIES $1.50 _____

24P . . HOW LOW INCOME COUNTRIES CAN ADVANCE THEIR OWN GROWTH $1.50 _____

23P . . MODERNIZING LOCAL GOVERNMENT $1.00 _____

22P . . A BETTER BALANCE IN FEDERAL TAXES ON BUSINESS 75¢ _____

21P . . BUDGETING FOR NATIONAL OBJECTIVES $1.00 _____

15P . . EDUCATING TOMORROW'S MANAGERS $1.00 _____

14P . . IMPROVING EXECUTIVE MANAGEMENT IN THE FEDERAL GOVERNMENT $1.50 _____

9P . . ECONOMIC LITERACY FOR AMERICANS 75¢ _____

1P . . ECONOMIC GROWTH IN THE UNITED STATES $1.00 _____

Quantity discounts: 10-24 copies—10%, 25-49 copies—15%, 50-99 copies—20%, 100-249 copies—30%

NOTE TO EDUCATORS: Instructors in colleges and universities may obtain
up to 5 free copies of those CED Statements on National Policy which they in-
tend to use in courses they are teaching. Please mention the course name when
ordering. For more than 5 copies, an educational discount of 20% will apply.

Course...

☐ I am enclosing $............................ for the copies ordered above.

☐ Please bill me. *(Payment must accompany orders under $10.00)*

DO YOU WANT ALL CED PUBLICATIONS WHEN ISSUED?

☐ I would like to obtain all CED publications as soon as they are issued. Please send
me information about the CED Reader Forum subscription plan.

☐ Please send me newest list of publications.

Name...

Organization...

Address...

City.. State.. Zip..

☐ **Businessman**   ☐ **Educator**   ☐ **Professional**

0534